C000299331

POET LUCK
1931–2007

A MEMOIR OUT OF THE ORDINARY

FOR JEAN,

MY WONDERFUL WIFE AND MY BEST FRIEND

POET LUCK
1931 – 2007

A MEMOIR OUT OF THE ORDINARY

Except for the public domain, this book is written solely from memory.
For that reason I append the letters at the foot of a traditional invoice:
E. & O. E., Errors and Omissions excepted.

First published in 2007 by Redcliffe Press Ltd.,
81g Pembroke Road, Bristol BS8 3EA

www.redcliffepress.co.uk
info@redcliffepress.co.uk

© Bill Pickard

ISBN 978-1-904537-73-1

British Library Cataloguing-in-Publication Data
A catalogue record for this book is available from the British Library

Typeset by Harper Phototypesetters Ltd, Northampton
Cover design by eandp, Bath wwweandp.co.uk
Printed by MPG Books, Bodmin, Cornwall

Contents

1	Pickards, Crofts And Others	1
2	Done Up To The Nines	10
3	Please Rain On My Parade	17
4	You Rang, My Lord?	26
5	Surprised By Joy	34
6	Kissing The Queen	40
7	Out Of The Strong (Came Forth Sweetness)	49
8	Wheels Within Wheels	58
9	The Good Soldier Pick	65
10	Five Fabulous Years	72
11	The Truth Shall Set You Free	82
12	Some Enchanted Evening	90
13	Waiting At The Church	99
14	For Art's Sake	109
15	Words, Words, Words	117
16	Go West, Young Man	129
17	Education, Education, Education	137
18	Not One Pomeranian Grenadier	145
19	I Do Like To Be Beside The Seaside	154
20	Nine Lives	162
21	The End, In Every Respect	168

The 48 poems between the chapters are taken from
Half A Ton: Selected Poems 1947–1997

Index	169

1

Pickards, Crofts and Others

Of my father's ancestors I can say only one thing with certainty. They originally came from Picardie in northern France, where the great cathedral of Amiens, the high point of Gothic architecture, towers over a city of Roman and pre-Roman origins.

Possibly, my father's folks came over to England with William the Conqueror. There were certainly Picards awarded lands in Wales by the Conqueror or by Odo of Bayeux who unveiled the Bayeux Tapestry in his Cathedral on 14th July 1077, exactly 712 years before Bastille Day, the hinge point of the French Revolution, and now the National Day of France.

It is equally possible that my paternal ancestors came to England as Huguenots, French Protestants who fled France after the revocation of the Edict of Nantes in 1685. King Louis XIV was a control freak, and one aspect of his control was religious. He saw Protestants as an affront to his national plans, and he wanted only Roman Catholics in his realm. King Louis XIV took away religious tolerance, and thousands of Huguenots fled to England, including many Picards. An historic affront to Rome was 'Picardy Prayers', silent prayers, so that only God knew what was prayed. As skilled craftsmen, Huguenots were fiercely independent, and they brought to England several skilled trades which are still traced to particular parts of London, such as Spitalfields and Soho. There is a French Protestant charity in Soho to this day.

The main clue to my father's family lies in most of his relatives being in Yorkshire. That makes 1066 arrival much more likely than 1685, as the historic reason for thousands of Yorkshire Pickards is the War of The Roses. The English Pickards were mainly Yorkists, and, after the Battle of Bosworth Field (1485) when Richard III was defeated and killed, the only safe place for Pickards to be was near to York, where they went.

Lancastrian Henry VII was too busy founding Tudor power in London to pursue the distant defeated Pickards. The vast majority of them are in Yorkshire to this day, including dozens of cousins whom I have never met.

My father's family include Benjamin Pickard (1842–1904) born at Kippax near Leeds, where I have many distant cousins. Benjamin, a coalpit worker from age 12 to age 31, was a West Yorkshire Miners' Association official from 1873 to 1876, becoming Secretary of W.Y.M.A. in 1876, and five years later, Secretary of the Yorkshire Miners' Association in 1881, ten years before my father was born. After the intervention of Lord Rosebery in the Great Strike of 1893, Benjamin Pickard became President of the Miners' Federation of Great Britain, and he had been the Member of Parliament for Normanton from 1885 to 1904, when he died at the age of 62 years. He was a radical M.P., and promoted 'The Eight Hours Bill' to limit miners' daily work hours, and other radical measures.

One of Benjamin's relatives, my father's father, Albert John Pickard married a Priestley cousin about 1880 and they had nine children, only four of whom survived, all boys. They were Albert (1889), William, my father (1891), John and Donald, known as Bert, Bill, Jack and Don. During their Great Yarmouth years they were known as many other things, including the Four Horsemen of the Apocalypse! From the 1890s to 1916 they were inseparable mates. For a very special reason. My grandfather had an uncle with no heir, and that uncle left grandad a seaside public house, The Queens Arms at Great Yarmouth.

Victoria's reign was ending, and her son looked forward to his reign, which would only be nine years (1901–1910), the Golden Age of the Edwardian Era. From 1910 onward Edward the VII's serious son, George V reigned 25 years over a Great Britain in the process of drastic changes.

But in the 1890s, when grandfather got the pub at Great Yarmouth, all was still Imperial greatness, calm and confidence. The sun seemed set to shine for ever. My grandfather made his

2

four sons an offer they could not refuse. They would work 21 days from dawn to dusk and then have 7 days' holiday, with a small handful of gold sovereigns THIRTEEN TIMES A YEAR for each son. For twenty years, until 1916, three sons were on duty at the pub and one was on holiday. How many company directors in the 21st century have thirteen weeks holiday a year? Periodically one son went off to London, Birmingham, Bristol, Manchester, Ireland, the Lake District, Cornwall, Glasgow, Edinburgh, or 'The Continent', with enough gold to 'live like a Lord'. I calculate that each son had 200 such holidays! A Golden Age.

My father had two rowboats, The Boy Billy (on the Norfolk Broads) and The Young Gunner, bought from the Army, for sea fishing. Thirty-nine weeks each year Dad was up at dawn to row out to his nets, pots and lines for hundreds of fish, which he gave to the pub or sold to the shops, and he saved the money. Dad was a great saver, a virtue he passed on.

Every four weeks, Dad took his sovereigns, packed his case, including evening dress wear, and set off for the big wide world, including Paris and the continental Low Countries, Brussels, Antwerp, Amsterdam, Rotterdam, Bruges. He was a 'Stage-Door Johnny' in the heyday of Edwardian music hall, and knew Marie Lloyd from her visits to Great Yarmouth, and all the music hall stars. His height was only 5'8" but his silk-lined cloak looked large, and his top hat took him over six feet tall. He was always a dandy, and for leisure wear sported a pussy bow, a willy hat and a come-to-Jesus collar. That was a floppy cravat tie (like Oscar Wilde) and a Homburg hat (like Kaiser Wilhelm) and a deep point-up collar. (Dandyism is contagious. When I earned my first few monthly salaries in 1947, at age 16, I bought a corduroy suit and a velour hat to match. I was then 6'2" and weighed 12 stones. It was the start of my seven years of dandyism).

In 1912 the unsinkable *Titanic* was sunk by an iceberg. In 1913 all Europe was restless, and in 1914 a chain of strange events led to the first World War. Great Yarmouth was part of the war zone. It was shelled by the German navy. By 1916 the war was not

3

going well for Britain, and Lord Derby introduced conscription for the armed forces. The cynical jingle went, "Lord Kitchener loves us, Lord Kitchener loves us, Lord Kitchener loves us – Lord Derby tells us so". Everywhere the posters of Lord Kitchener pointed at British men. 'YOUR COUNTRY NEEDS YOU' was the message.

Grandfather was about 60 years of age so he decided to retire to a country cottage, and the four sons, including my father, all joined the forces. Bert and Don joined the Navy. Dad and Jack joined the Army. My father's skill at catering took him to Northern Command, centred on York, where he spent three years catering for thousands of soldiers. While he was at York, he met my mother, Emily Croft, probably the best thing that ever happened to him.

Of my mother's ancestors I know very little. My grandmother's family name was Horsley, and her father was multi-talented, ranging from playing cricket for Yorkshire to being a superbly skilled bootmaker to Yorkshire gentry. His speciality was knee length riding boots.

From the 1870s onwards he was licensee of the Lord Nelson public house, in the village of Poppleton, near York, and near the Bishopthorpe Palace where the Archbishops of York live. The gardens of the Lord Nelson slope down to the river, and for much of the year York people and holidaymakers boat down the river Ouse to spend a refreshing few hours in the pub gardens. Three of my grandmother's brothers are remembered on the Poppleton war memorial. One was called Marmaduke, always known as 'Duke'. My grandmother, Edith was one of a dozen children, only one of whom died in childhood.

Edith Horsley was one of the youngest children, and a very naughty girl. She hatched a plan to marry the tall (6'4") handsome only son of the local magnate, named Croft, who managed London and North Eastern Railway matters at York, and lived in a very large house at Poppleton. Edith seduced George Henry Stephen Croft, and then told him of her pregnancy. George was supposed to 'claim his inheritance' early, and become a mini-magnate with Edith his wife. George was a great 'catch'. He was public school-educated, and a talented musician.

The teenage Edith's plan misfired. Croft Senior was angry and outraged by his son's behaviour, as he had arranged for George to be interviewed by Sir Charles Villiers Stanford, Professor of Music at Cambridge University, a plan which had to be abandoned. George's father told him to marry Edith, and that he would always have a good job with LNER, but that was all. Unambitious George was quite content. He was a fine pianist, he sung in York Minster Choir and occasionally played church organs.

George and Edith were married in 1899, and Lucy was born soon after. My mother, Emily, was born in 1901 and George Oswald was born in 1915. He was a brilliant boy, who became one of ICI's top pharmacists. George and Edith were a devoted couple, who each lived to a great age. My grandfather used to take me for walks around York, and across Knavesmire, where the race course is. He also took me to the village of Heslington, where the new York University now stands, and I still have his walking stick that we used to hook branches of blackberries, and eat them.

My mother was one of York's beauties. She had very dark hair and eyes, perfect skin and a superb figure. She was very tall for a girl, and got a job in Leek and Thorp's Emporium as a sales girl and fashion model. She had a calm temper, and was a Christian believer from nine years old, having been converted by an Evangelist's Mission in 1910. In her teens she received several proposals of marriage, from some of York's richest young (and not so young) men. She prayed about each proposal, and did not accept any of them. She was waiting for Mr. Right.

In 1919, a year after the War ended, my father was waiting to be demobilised from the Army. He was still a catering officer at Northern Command Headquarters, Fulford Barracks, because he was thought indispensable. Apart from his Army friends, Dad had a cousin at Bradford, J.B. Priestley, who was three years younger than father. John Boynton Priestley was at the start of his literary career. Twenty years later, by the Second World War, JBP was a world-famous novelist, playwright and broadcaster who gave inspiring radio talks to wartime Britain.

One day in 1919 Priestley contacted my father urgently. He had been due to take a lady to a fashion show at Leek and Thorp's Emporium but could not fulfil the engagement. Would my father please escort the lady? Father agreed. He was not busy, and life was rather routine. In Army terms, he was marking time. A typical day brought a telegram from a regimental adjutant – "My men complain that their tea is dried tea leaves". Father's reply was "With respect, Sir, all tea is dried tea leaves". The problems of peace.

Dressed in his best, my father escorted the lady to the fashion show. Even in 1919, some women spent £1,000 a year on dresses and tailored clothing, equivalent to a £1,000 a week nowadays. Father sat among those wealthy women and their escorts. Suddenly he sat straight and took notice. A tall, beautiful, dark-haired girl walked a dress past them and away again. Then she modelled some more dresses, and father was pink with pleasure. Who ever loved who loved not at first sight? Within a week he had met Emily Croft, and taken her to dine after her working day. By New Year 1920 they were engaged. Soon after, father left the Army, and sat Civil Service exams, becoming a tax officer, Inland Revenue. He was 28 years old, his fiancée was 18, but so what? In those days it was normal for such an age gap in marriage.

The only Inland Revenue job available to him was in London, so he rented a flat in Camden Hill Road, Upper Norwood, and they wrote six letters a week, three each way, for almost two years, while they saved their money for the great adventure of marriage. In February 1922, when he was 30 and she was 20, they were married at St. Clements Church, York, early on a weekday morning, to avoid a crowd. Four hundred people attended the wedding, and a few pursued them to their change of train to cover them in confetti at Doncaster station. After their honeymoon near

6

Great Yarmouth, they lived in Camden Hill Road until 1929, when they secured a Lambeth council house at 42 Salters Hill, Upper Norwood facing on to Norwood Park, hundreds of acres of lovely parkland, with every facility for healthy recreation. They waited on the council housing list for seven years to get the exact house that they wanted, at the crest of the hill, facing on to a beautiful park. So happy were they in that house, that they never even thought of moving elsewhere. They each died in their sleep, in that house of a thousand memories. Father died in 1970, aged 79, and mother died in 1983, aged 82, sleeping in her favourite chair. When mother died my brother John and I found 54 years of rent books, all weekly receipted. We worked out that our parents paid less than £5,000 total rent for 54 years of happy housing. That sum included all repairs, updates, repaints (in and out), wallpapering, immersion heaters, new fireplaces, new baths, and, in wartime, several replacements of windows and two new roofs. All that, including rent and rates, for less than £2 per week. Lambeth Borough has had some doubtful decades recently, but in the half century from 1930 it must have been one of the best in Britain.

My brother, Albert John Priestley Pickard, was born in 1924, and had an emergency appendix operation in 1929, the year of the move to Salters Hill. A strong constitution and Norwood Park soon had him well again. But his parents had had a scare. They had no spare baby, and he had no brother or sister. They set about some serious mating, and, glory be, a back-up baby was conceived on a hot night in June 1930. The rest, as they say, is history! The one that follows.

For my father and Thomas Hardy

HEROINES

Nothing is asked of heroes, but that they
Have heroines. No more is asked than that.
Two men I treasure had so many such
That all the reaching of their arms and pens
Could not contain them. Women, shrined on shelves,
Out of men's minds, out of their very selves.

They never met. Perhaps they're meeting now,
With all of time to sit down and discuss
Tess on her final journey to Stonehenge,
Bathsheba Everdene being a wilful child,
Eustacia Vye blazing like a heath fire,
The victims, and the causes, of desire.

Then they'll discuss some women not in books,
And shake their heads, still sadly unaware
Of what it is (or Who) makes women tick.
Reach out your arms. For real or paper love.
My father says, "The man who kids himself
He understands a woman, kids himself."

THE VERB "TO BE"
CAN HAVE NO OBJECT

More often than folks ask
After my health
Or wealth, they ask me,
Seemingly sincere
"What do you want?"

The nursery teacher
Kneeling at my side
Attained my size
But not my sympathy,
"What do you want?"

The kind headmaster
Forehead sadly creased,
Said, "You could be a soldier
Or a priest.
What do you want?"

My first true love
Thought she had given all.
Perhaps she had,
And yet her eyes reproached,
"What do you want?"

I'd like to answer
Something they could write
Into a book, To tell them
When they look,
"That's what he wants".

He only wants to BE,
No more, no less;
Wants nothing but to be –
And that precludes
Defining other want.

2

Done Up To The Nines

By teatime on 9th March 1931 my mother was fed up with being urged to "Puuush". Not that she was too posh to push, but she had been in labour with me for several hours. I was the problem. I was LARGE. The midwife at the nursing home on Knights Hill, West Norwood felt professionally challenged. She guessed that I weighed ten pounds. It was a good guess. Close.

Finally, at about five p.m., a loud noise signalled my arrival, just as my father was walking up Knights Hill from West Norwood railway station. It was the same Knights Hill that Camille Pissarro, the French Impressionist painted in 1870 when he was avoiding the Prussian invasion of France and the Siege of Paris. During his brief exile, Pissarro painted many views of Norwood, South London.

There was only time for nurses to clean me up, weigh my nine pounds nine ounces, and settle me in mother's arms, as my father arrived, with flowers. I was still making a noise. I made it for several days. It was "A-laa, A-laa, A-laa", which a tactful nurse said sounded aristocratic. After nine years of marriage, on the ninth day of March, William and Emily had produced a second son, nine pounds nine ounces of boy. My father was impressed by my size and my noise. "That's right, you tell 'em," he said, as he held me close to his face, "You tell 'em."

It was the first of thousands of conversations we had in my thirty-nine years before he died. We were always talking, or reciting poems, or singing folk songs or music hall songs or Salvation Army hymns or Gilbert's words to Sullivan's music. Anything with a good tune to it. But not opera. We drew the line at opera. Whenever father heard opera he said, "My God, he (or she) has got his head stuck. Fetch the Fire Brigade."

Father suggested to mother that such a super child deserved to have his full names, and she agreed. A few days later I was registered as William Priestley Pickard, exactly like father. When they took me home to 42 Salters Hill, I was still saying "A-laa, A-laa, A-laa", but not continuously. Just for a short spell every waking hour. I was also looking around, and varying the tone of short cries, happy, sad, good and bad. A full dramatic range.

I was given the big back bedroom. Not because of my bulk, but because my brother, nearly seven years old, had specially chosen the small front bedroom. It was only half the size of my bedroom, but it had windows overlooking the road and the park, and a distant view of the institution where Charlie Chaplin and his brother had been placed when their mother was very ill and very poor. Brother John loved his small side window, where he could see passers-by, and the bright red buses on Central Hill, creeping to Crystal Palace, and its long wide Parade, their terminus. Downhill buses dashed to Streatham and London's West End. That was Route 137. Buses on Route 2 went to West Norwood, Tulse Hill, Brixton, Stockwell, Vauxhall, Victoria, Park Lane, and Golders Green. Route 2 was the oldest route on London Transport, because Route 1 had been changed. Two of the oddest incidents of my life involved buses on Route 2. So much for brother John's observations from his room.

My bedroom had one large window above the back garden, an upward slope, where my father's large-gauge model railway followed the fences, and came into the small downstairs room at head high, through a transom window. Except at the top of the garden the railway ran on wooden viaducts, up to six feet above the ground and strong enough to bear my weight on a saddle-truck pulled by any of the three large locomotives. I had many years of pleasure from that railway. The station, controls, carriages and trucks were all in a wooden shed, and the Station had a complete tableau on its roof, with a sign "Married above his Station". It was all in superb Bassett-Lowke stock, from their splendid shop at the west end of Holborn, opposite Holborn underground and tramway stations. For five years, from age eleven, I would go to school at the east end of Holborn, almost opposite Gamages' great department store, founded by the seventeenth child of poor parents from Hereford. The only greater emporium was Harrods in Knightsbridge, set up in 1849 to catch the expected Grocery Trade for the millions attending the Great Exhibition in 1851. Mr. Harrod, from London's East End, rented a small shop near Hyde Park. Today it is a massive market, perhaps the most famous in all the world. Small men, big dreams.

I was a very little man, with no dreams at all. I never dream. The garden below my bedroom window had a large lawn, ending at a summerhouse covered in honeysuckle and a fence heavy with brambles, which fruited blackberries richly every autumn. My bedroom was even larger than my parents' front bedroom, and I had it for all twenty five years that I lived at home, and during all my visits in later years, sometimes with my wife and daughters. For all my first sixteen years before I went to work, I had to be in my room by an appropriate bedtime, but, once there, I could read or write or draw or paint. I also had an ever-augmented set of metal Meccano to make models. It had a little motor, so some were working models. My Meccano fed into my later passion for bicycles. In my 21st-century shed (110 square feet) I have a hand-built tricycle and five bicycles, all the objects of much mechanical delight.

Before midnight in my boyhood room, I put away all toys in the huge wooden toybox below the window, and prepared for sleep. When tiny I needed ten hours sleep, when small I needed eight hours, but by teenage I managed on six hours sleep. Two hours per day "saved" from sleep add up to ten whole years extra living (10x365x24 hours or 87,600 extra hours to be active). Time, and its use, was a parental obsession upon me. I had to be moving forward by the hour. One of father's odd sayings was "Never come out of a room the same person as you went in". On pre-war railway stations there were slot machines telling your weight for a penny. Father's attitude was adamant, "Why waste a penny on weight when you can buy chocolate, and weigh a bit more". Physically and mentally, I was always expected to 'weigh a bit more'. I never had comics but I was given many books, and I was a competent reader at three, fluent at five. By six or seven years I read my parents' newspapers and magazines, and discussed things with them. For bodily growth I was well fed, and I had a large park opposite for games and sports. I also had the huge grounds of the Crystal Palace to explore.

I was given a tricycle at two, and a bicycle at four years. By six years I had a larger bike and at eight a larger geared cycle. It was big enough to be usable until I was eleven years old and sixty-six inches tall and seven stone. I was always taller and heavier than contemporaries. From six years I was allowed supervised cycling on roads, which in the 1930s had few cars. By the time (late 1939) I was sent to the country I was cycling ten miles frequently, and my bike was essential in the country, for reasons I shall tell. Mag and Fred, two colleagues of my father, had a touring tandem bicycle with sidecar, and they often took me into the heart of Surrey and Kent for whole days. Between breakfast time and tea time we covered fifty, sixty or more miles. Once they took me to Brighton, a round ride of one hundred miles. Most important of all, they took me to Herne Hill Cycle Stadium, at the edge of Dulwich, and that stadium became one of the influences upon my life. I saw all the famous track cyclists of Europe, some of whom were killed in World War II. I saw eighteen-year-old Reg Harris race against the world's best, before being called into the Army. After being wounded in north Africa, Reg Harris came back to be several times world champion in the 1940s and 1950s. He was influential in my life in 1948, London Olympic Games Year.

Salters Hill Primary School was at the foot of Norwood Park, beyond the railway line, and stretched along Gipsy Road, opposite a row of shops. One of those shops was a sweetshop where I used to spend my earnings as a playground boxing promoter in 1938 and 1939. I had noticed that some boys wanted to fight other boys. I had also noticed that these cruel contests were wild and unskilled. I had a book of boxing rules and a wristwatch. My scheme was simple. Each boy gave me one penny (the old penny was worth 2½ new pennies) and the winner received one and a half pennies, leaving me with a half-penny per fight. I used to spend all those in the sweetshop to grow bigger.

Salters Hill School was an ugly red-brick building, and was as basic inside as it was outside. I was there from five to eight and a half, when I was sent to the Surrey countryside for the first three years of the War. I had to go where my big brother's secondary school went. I never saw my schoolmates again, and I remember no master's name. Thanks to my home education, I was already writing verse, for which I had great facility. I have always been more ready to write verse than prose, and, seventy years on, that is still the case. My parents had given me hundreds of books, including some collections of poetry, such as Palgrave's Golden Treasury. Of my present seven thousand books, about two thousand are of poetry, and I always read more.

One of my father's favourite poems, which we used to say together, was 'A Boy's Song' by James Hogg, the Ettrick shepherd born in the Scottish borders in the same year that Wordsworth was born in Cockermouth, Cumbria, 1770. 'A Boy's Song' has only six four-line verses, and each verse ends, "That's the way for Billy and me". My father was a Billy and I am a Billy, and on Sunday mornings we used stride out together, hand in hand, saying "Up the river and o'er the lea, That's the way for Billy and me". The second verse says:

Where the blackbird sings the latest,
Where the hawthorn blooms the sweetest,
Where the nestlings chirp and flee,
That's the way for Billy and me.

When I was eleven, and far from home, a hawthorn tree figured in one of the great events of my life. At the time I did not think it was one of the 'sweetest', but looking back, it may have been.

ROUTINE

The morn
Is sometimes full of hope.
I yawn,
But the abyss does not.

I leap from bed,
And do not grope
My way about,
But, flinging wide
The window, sing
A song of praise.

Some days, however,
Man will not be loved,
God will not be revealed,
The theorem
Will not be proved;
The breach
Refuses to be healed.

On such a day of pain
Routine
Will keep me sane.

When other lovers fail me
With a glimpse
Of what might have been,
O, come to my arms,
Obligation.
Come, rest on my breast,
Routine.

COMING OF AGE

On Saturday August Sixth,
Transfiguration Day,
The twenty-first anniversary
Of the Hiroshima Bomb,
The President's daughter
Was married amid
Seven hundred guest,
Three thousand troops,
And dozens of detectives.

During the honeymoon
Every third cherub
On the bedpost
Was a microphone.
Not only was the bed bugged,
Their footsteps were dogged.
Everything possible for their
Health and happiness
Had been thought of.

But their real satisfaction
Came from the sackfuls
Of greetings received.
Some were: Happy twentyfirst,
Loving wishes from Saigon,
May nothing ever Hanoi you
And
May all your fallouts
Be little ones.

3

Please Rain On My Parade

The subtitle of this book is 'A Memoir out of the Ordinary'. As with the book's main title, I like words that can be taken more than one way. My early years were certainly 'out of the ordinary', near to some people far from ordinary. The Bloomhall Housing Estate at Upper Norwood was wonderfully sited, but not architecturally remarkable. They were ordinary houses, rented for less than ten shillings a week (50 pence) in the 1930s. At Winchelsea and other places are council estates that win prizes, but not at Norwood. There, it was the people who won prizes. In my road lived a girl who married a millionaire. She won a scholarship to St. Martin's School, Tulse Hill, and she was both bright and beautiful. How or when she met her millionaire I do not know, but all at Salters Hill knew on the many occasions when his Rolls-Royce car was parked outside her home, and we all rejoiced when they wed. She was a local heroine. Only one of many.

Two doors away from my parents lived a family where one man ran a restaurant, one girl founded a travel agency, and another daughter married the Police Chief of New Zealand. That amazing family gave me a superb leather bound bible when I went to theological college at age twenty five. The bible had four columns, 1611 Authorised Version, 1881 Revised Version, Hebrew (39 Old Testament) and Greek (27 NT Books) and a blank column for student notes. A small library. Next door to my parents lived the Superintendent of West Norwood Tram Depot, who managed a fleet of trams on routes as far away as Holborn Subway. When I started at Mercers' School in 1942, I used to travel by tram to Holborn Subway every weekday for two old pence (less than one new penny). The West Norwood Tram Terminus was a dead-end outside St. Luke's Church, one of the four famous 'Waterloo Churches', built to honour the British victory at the Battle of

Waterloo, Belgium, in 1815. The other three Waterloo Churches are St. John's, Waterloo Road, where I have attended many events, St. Matthew's, Brixton, where I had occasional Ministry in the 1960s, and St. Mark's, Kennington, near the Oval test cricket ground, and Surrey C.C.C. headquarters. Our next-door neighbour's trams passed all those churches, and he was a good neighbour.

A few yards away from his tram terminus were the large front gates of West Norwood Cemetery, the dead end of many thousands, and last resting place of some famous folk. Norwood Cemetery was opened in 1837 when the teenage Queen Victoria began her reign. In its grounds it had a Greek Cemetery (full of merchant millionaires) and a small German Cemetery for the pre-1914 German community at Sydenham and Forest Hill, below the Crystal Palace. They had their own church. The French had no specific part of Norwood Cemetery but some are there. Famous Britons abound in that ground. Charles Haddon Spurgeon, powerful preacher at the Baptist Tabernacle, had many thousands at his funeral there. Thousands more lined the streets to West Norwood. Tom King and Tom Spring were both boxing champions of England. The ancestor of my first bosses Sir Henry Tate (sugar and picture galleries), Jeremiah Coleman (mustard), Sir Henry Doulton (pottery), Stoughton of Hodder and Stoughton (books), Sir Henry Bessemer (steel process), several Lord Mayors of London, many bankers, many actors, and Sir Hiram Maxim (machine guns) who used to leaflet his West Norwood neighbours of the days and times he would be firing machine guns in his back garden. A perfect gentleman. Last, but not least, the famous Mrs Beeton (Victorian domestic goddess) who died at 29 years of age. Norwood Cemetery is a jolly jaunt, on a wet Wednesday.

Our other next-door neighbour had a career in heavy transport for Watneys Brewery at Mortlake on Thames, overlooking the finish of the Oxford versus Cambridge Boat Races every spring. Chiswick Bridge (and the boat houses) are just beyond, and every year, after the finish, one crew of nine Giants celebrate, and nine nobodies all collapse like punctured balloons. I saw it at Mortlake eighteen times, and every year since on television. Our Watney's Brewery neighbour became transport manager, and moved to a big house near the Thames, within walking distance from his work. Next door to him, the only daughter married her boss, the continental travel manager of Southern Railway, who had a big office on Victoria Station, starting point for the famous 'Golden Arrow' train. Their honeymoon was in Paris and beyond.

Two doors further along Salters Hill lived a family whose father was assistant manager of an Austin Reed, Gentlemen's Outfitters, where I used to buy my shirts by the half dozen. His elder son became Principal of a teacher training college and his younger son had his own jeweller's shops, and designed jewellery. He made my wife's ruby and gold engagement ring, and also our wedding ring. So far, I have mentioned nine remarkable people in five houses.

From only five council houses, I have listed nine remarkable people, and I only knew one small corner of the Estate. Was it all like that? A hundred high flyers? All their memoirs would be out of the ordinary.

On a more sombre note, 1936 got off to a sad start. King George V died in January, worried about the behaviour of his elder son and heir, Edward, with various married women, but especially the American, Mrs Wallis Simpson. Small wonder that the King's doctors suggested that sea air at Bognor Regis would ease his ills. The King replied, "Bugger Bognor". And died soon after. A few days after the King died, Rudyard Kipling (poet, essayist, novelist, short story genius and children's book writer) also died. Some newspapers unkindly remarked, "King George has gone and he has taken his trumpeter with him". Kipling was overly Imperial, but had atoned for sending his teenage son to die in the war trenches in France. Kipling's atonement was to be responsible for those vast memorial cemeteries in France and Flanders, where one of the headstones is for his son John. With all Kipling's faults, no less a literary judge than the poet T.S. Eliot said of him "I have

19

never met a man of more complete genius". When Kipling's critics are long dead, his written works will still be supreme. Perhaps for ever.

Soon after George and Rudyard departed, I had a birthday with five candles on the cake. I also started school, and found it incredibly easy, far less study than imposed by my parents. I had read all the nursery classics, and at five was beginning to read real stories, and looking things up in a *Children's Encyclopaedia*. In 1937, 1938 and 1939 I added to my reading *Masterman Ready*, *The Water Babies*, *Children of the New Forest*, and the works of Arthur Ransome, A.A. Milne, and the historical novels of G.A. Henty. Other historical fiction included the novels of Baroness Orczy (*Scarlet Pimpernel*, etc.) and also some heavy history in *Foxe's Book of Martyrs*. Religion has always underpinned history, so it is not surprising that I found the Reformation and the Civil War of interest. After 'Foxe', reading *Mein Kampf* (Hitler's quasi-religious book) was a light relief. Few people except Winston Churchill realised what Hitler's quasi-religion was doing to Germany. In the 1980s I spent a half hour coach break looking at the house-prison in Bavaria where Hitler <u>dictated</u> his book to disciple Rudolph Hess. Charlie Chaplin exposed in his 1940 film *The Great Dictator* what figures of farce Hitler and Mussolini were. Also evil. The definition of farce is 'Tragedy, happening to other people'.

By the autumn of 1936 all Britain was concerned about the playboy King Edward. Would he ever shape up? The Prime Minister Stanley Baldwin (Kipling's cousin) was worried. Winston Churchill was worried. Lord Beaverbrook was worried. The playboy Prince didn't want to be King. Nor did he want to admit that. Mrs. Simpson wanted to be Queen, but that was ruled out. She became the perfect excuse for Edward to abdicate, but October dragged in to November, and on the last night of November 1936 something serious happened....

The Crystal Palace burned down. How do glass and metal burn? But they did, and the flames seemed to assault my bedroom

20

window, hundreds of yards away. On the first of December it was all over. A hundred fire engines, a thousand fire men, a million observers, were all powerless to stop it. I wanted rain. Please rain on my Parade, the Crystal Palace Parade. My dream-Palace had stood there for more than eighty years, since it was transferred to a hill above Sydenham after the Great Exhibition in Hyde Park ended in 1851. For more than eighty years the greatest galas, the greatest concerts, the greatest fireworks were only at the Crystal Palace. The fireworks excelled themselves that night, and by December's dawn it was finished. (Except for one tower by Anerley Hill, which stood till it was destroyed by Royal Engineers in the War, because it was guiding enemy aircraft.) There are many theories about the Crystal Palace fire. The most plausible is that the many miles of dry wooden planks which were the flooring, and eighty years of dry dust down below these planks, were accidentally ignited. A boiler? A cigarette-end? A wire? Nobody knows, but it was destroyed in a few hours.

I knelt on my toy-box looking at the fireball on the hill. Ash and smoke reached as far as our garden, and when the centre span of the Palace collapsed inward, flames belched half a mile into the sky. It was a lantern for ten miles around. It was visible from fifty miles away. I was crying in my bedroom. Millions of Londoners mourned the passing of a friend. There were heart failures that night in people who were not as old as the Crystal Palace. When stupid schemes such as the Millennium Dome at Greenwich were being projected, I wrote to many at Westminster to rebuild the Crystal Palace on its original site, using indestructible materials. I never had a reply to any of my letters. A millionaire Texan property developer plans to duplicate the Crystal Palace as an exhibition centre at Dallas. Its frontage will be much shorter at only 400 feet, but it will climb fifteen storeys into the sky, and it will take twice as long to build. I await news of the finished result.

The trauma of that night in 1936 had a permanent effect upon me. It made me distrust all alleged material certainties. But it gave a loophole to King Edward. Within days he determined to abdicate the throne of Great Britain and marry Mrs. Wallis Simpson. Edward found a big event (the Palace fire) in which to bury his broadcast abdication. It rates less in history than Neville Chamberlain's Munich piece of paper, and far less than the same man's broadcast of the start of World War Two. Small boys like me also had a new carol that December, bellowed without reverence:

Hark the Herald Angels sing
Mrs. Simpson's pinched our King ...

The year 1937 saw a new King, George VI from whose Coronation I still have some posh crockery. The grounds of the Crystal Palace reopened, and life continued much as before. Without my beloved Palace my parents took me to many places in London – The British Museum (awesome), The Science Museum (put me off for life), Victoria and Albert Museum (I loved it), Imperial War Museum (aeroplanes hanging from the roof), Horniman's Museum (with a bisected cat in a glass case, decades before Damien Hirst's artworks). When I went to Madame Tussaud's Waxworks, I was reminded that her first house in England was only four hundred yards from where I lived. I walked past it daily, where the refugee from France brought her death masks and wax equipment after the French Revolution and the guillotine Terror.

When I was shown a Grecian Urn in the British Museum my father told me of John Keats' famous poem, 'Ode On A Grecian Urn'. To this day, I can see the frieze of figures frozen in time. My parents took me to theatres, cinemas and concert halls. I can remember, at age six, seeing and hearing 'Hiawatha', the Samuel Coleridge-Taylor musical setting of Longfellow's great poem. When I was offering dozens of different literary courses, forty years later, 'Hiawatha' was one of the most popular courses, equally so in primary schools, secondary schools, colleges and art centres. Hiawatha is both historic and timeless.

In 1938 I had my first seaside holiday, at Hemsby in Norfolk. Our village of chalets had a General Store & Post Office where the radio was reporting an eighteen-year-old man from Yorkshire scoring 364 runs in a Test Match at the Kennington Oval. Len Hutton was a lad from the area where all my ancestors came from, the Bradford/Leeds conurbation. His Test Match record score stood for decades, until Brian Lara, of the West Indies, beat it.

Throughout 1939 we all knew that war was a possibility, and discussion with my father indicated that there were two opinions of Neville Chamberlain, the Prime Minister. Some thought him a weak appeaser, with his Munich piece of paper. Others thought him a clever buyer of time for Britain to build up wartime resources. I had read Hitler's book *Mein Kampf*, and I tended to the clever time-buyer view. After all, one does not aggravate a mad dog. Hitler, between the Wars was very mad, but also clever. It is the German people of the 1920s and 1930s I wonder about. Would Britons ever support such a leader? I hope not, but if one is slowly gulled, as they were, one can get beyond a point of no return before realising it.

By August 1939, the twenty-fifth anniversary of the start of World War One, another war seemed likely. Hitler's troops were moving into neighbouring territory, and Britain set him a deadline for better behaviour. There was no response. On the morning of Sunday 3rd September 1939, I listened, with my family, to Neville Chamberlain's broadcast of Britain being in a state of war. At least, he had bought us more than a year of preparation time.

DUST TO DUST

A dozen kinds of creatures
Lose their homes,
A dozen fields
Are swallowed up in one,
And, on a sunny
Summer afternoon,
The earth is raped.

They cannot answer back,
The planners say –
Birds on the wing
No longer need a bush
In which to hide
Their quite outdated heads.
Nature is starved.

Quite soon enough
When profits start to fall
To think about
The wisdom of it all:
To wonder
Where the planners have gone wrong.
When profits slide.

Quite time enough
When miles of dusty dirt,
The wastes of Warwick
And Northamptonshire
Are deserts
Where not even grass will grow.
A land that died.

FRAMED

I view the picture in its light oak frame,
And think, "Could that be me as recently
As that hot Summer, just three years ago?"
"I paint you now" she said, "just as you are"
(That's an illusion, if there ever was)
"For you will never be the same again."

That much is true. The differences show.
She painted me, and put me in a frame,
And gave it to me as a reminder. But
Of what she did not say. I do not need
To be reminded of that Summer, nor
Of anything so recent. Nor do I

Need to be framed. Take every frame away
And let my outer edges touch all Space,
And let my face both look and be
Part of a galaxy. No telescope
Is capable of focussing on love,
And no computer software programmes hope.

There are too many frames; and every one
Is holding countless precious freedoms in
Like prisoners. Some frames are families,
Some are examinations, social norms,
Professional associations,
Walking and talking dead "freemasonries".

Even the waking dead lie down some day,
And Someone says they need no more get up,
No more tell lies, no more conceal the truth,
No more of humbug and hypocrisy.

Jude the Obscure could surely not be blamed
For carving on a headstone, "He was framed".

4

You Rang, My Lord?

In December 1936 we had the radio broadcast of the abdication of King Edward VIII. In September 1939 we had a broadcast notification of a state of war between Britain and Germany.

In 1940, my father's cousin, J.B. Priestley, gave a series of 21 short broadcasts to the nation, known as 'Postscripts'. They were always at 9.15pm, a time when whole families could listen. The first broadcast, on Wednesday 5th June 1940 was directly related to the retreat (by sea) from Dunkirk in France. It was about the motley fleet of ships and boats that plucked an army from under the noses and the guns of German power. Many were pleasure steamers, some were wooden 'Skylarks' that took holidaymakers round the lighthouse at seaside resorts, for a shilling, many were private amateur boats never before seriously used. Priestley ended his talk with the words, "And our grandchildren, when they learn how we began this war by snatching glory out of defeat, and then swept on to Victory, may also learn how the little holiday steamers made an excursion to Hell, and came back glorious."

That broadcast was exactly four years before the huge D-Day fleet sailed across to France, the greatest Armada in history, on the 6th June 1944. What faith J.B. Priestley showed in that first broadcast. There had been months of the 'Phoney War' when the British mainland seemed immune from danger. Was Hitler asleep? Neville Chamberlain's paperchase, and the Phoney War gave almost two years of preparation time for the British industries relevant to war. Metal objects from an ounce to several tons were being donated to the war effort. Park railings and house railings, pots and pans, old bikes, motorbikes and cars were given as scrap metal. Other vital schemes, 'Dig for Victory' (the home-grown food campaign), protection of all glass in buildings and buses, blackout of all windows that might show a light to bombers. Air raid wardens, puffed with power, Heavy Rescue (who seemed to be small men) and Light Rescue (who seemed bigger men), Local Defence Volunteers (later, the Home Guard, "Dad's Army"), and dozens of special small units of defence were mobilised additional to their daily work. A cartoon character called Billy Brown of London Town warned all bus passengers: "I trust you'll pardon my correction, That stuff is there for your protection!" To which the bus passenger (allegedly) replied, "Thank you for your information, But now I've missed my bloody station." Everyone carried a cardboard box containing their gas mask. Rich people had polished leather gas mask boxes. I had a military steel helmet, bought by my parents. At the height of the Blitz it saved my life.

After Dunkirk, Goering's air armada against Britain began, initially to destroy our aerodromes and planes, the famous Battle of Britain, up to the autumn 1940. Then the blanket bombing of London and other cities, to destroy factories, businesses and the morale of the civilian population.

Four days after his first broadcast 'Postscript', J.B. Priestley began a Sunday evening series from 9th June to 20th October 1940. He began the last one with the words, "This is my last Sunday Postscript for some time, perhaps the last I shall ever do." He then referred to the success of our fighters in the Battle of Britain, and the endurance of the Blitz by civilians. He ended the last broadcast with "thanks for the thousands of pleasant letters, for all manner of little kindnesses and expressions of gratitude, and for listening. I'll always be proud to remember how many times I caught your ear as we all marched through the blitzkrieg together. It might have been worse, mightn't it?"

Just 21 ten minute talks, yet some consider them the best short talks ever broadcast. Certainly, they caught the mood, conveying that we were all in the struggle together. That is my most powerful impression of 1939–1945, the assumed and acted unity of us all. Sadly, it faded fast after the war ended.

One of the great National Plans was to send children of school age out of any area likely to attract enemy bombers. The word was 'evacuee', and there were hundreds of thousands of us. For the first time in our lives, my brother and I had to be aware of our linked destinies, at least until he became sixteen and took employment. He was only one year short of leaving school, but in 1940 we were a common problem for one country family. I say 'country', but where we were sent was not obviously country. I had to go where my brother's secondary school was sent, and that was to Leatherhead in Surrey, only 20 miles from home, and on a train line to Tulse Hill, with frequent electric trains. Such a suburban location was probably chosen because most of my brother's schoolmates would soon be old enough for employment. (My school meanwhile, with children from five to eleven years old, was sent 200 miles west.)

I was the only primary aged boy attached to my brother's school, and became a problem for billeting officers. Soon after the start of the war we travelled with our basic possessions to Leatherhead. My mother had supplied me with several pairs of long trousers, then not usual for eight-year olds, because I was so big I would look silly in short trousers. In size and interests I was much closer to the eleven- and twelve-year olds at my brother's school, and they became my spare-time companions. Two days of door-to-door billeting attempts failed to find a foster home for me and my brother. Each evening we were temporarily lodged in a large house south of Leatherhead, on the Dorking side. It was a clearing centre for boys not yet placed. By the third day, only a few teenage boys and myself were unplaced. My brother was fifteen-years old and quite tall. It suited me to be with him and his con-temporaries. In the evening I went into the radio room of the large house, where there were comfortable chairs, some shelves of books, and a solitary newspaper. It was a *Daily Express*, and I was quietly reading it when a rugged little man, like a stone gargoyle, came in. He saw what I was reading, and he mentioned one or two matters in the newspaper. As I responded, he showed interest, and we chatted for a long time. He seemed to be sounding and testing me. I told him my schooling was a problem, as I was one alone in my age-group. He learned some of my interests, and then said he could solve my school problem. Would my parents agree to his plan? As he needed to know, I gave him one of several stamped, addressed envelopes my mother had given me, so that I would write home regularly. He copied the name and address, and returned my envelope, saying that he would contact my parents. The next day he sent someone to 42 Salters Hill, and it was agreed that I should go to a small private school, and that he would pay all fees and expenses during my Leatherhead years.

I discovered that my small rugged friend was Lord Beaverbrook, the proprietor of the *Daily Express*. He told me where I could contact him, and my bicycle was sent to me on the same day that my brother and I were placed. It had spare tyres, tubes and a saddlebag added for long-term use. Not one need had been neglected. Next day, my brother and I were accepted by a middle-aged couple who lived at the edge of Leatherhead, near the golf course. They lived in a cul-de-sac, leading to fields where cows grazed. Strangely, I don't think I saw a cultivated field in all my three years at Leatherhead, only grass and woodland.

My foster parents, Arthur and Lilian, lived in a semi-detached modern house which they owned. He was a builders' foreman, and had a garage workshop beside the house. The back garden was like a market garden, with all fruits and vegetables, and an orchard of apple trees. They also had a dozen chickens in a large hen run. Their dog, Rex was a black terrier about three years old, and trained to hunt rabbits. In fact, my first task was to spend the evening helping to make half-inch lead balls for a very powerful catapult which Arthur gave me. He could always obtain scrap lead from the sites where he worked, and we made about a hundred lead balls a week, with a mould. Arthur knew all the rabbit runs, and we sent Rex round behind green cover to flush out the rabbits towards us. Arthur's catapult shots were often successful, but it took me weeks of practice on static targets before I could hit the head of a running rabbit. Arthur always brought two rabbits home, and often more. These were either eaten or traded for rare and rationed items. By bartering their produce Arthur and Lilian always had a full larder. I have never eaten so well as I did during my three years at Leatherhead. I grew visibly month by month, eating hugely and bicycling miles to school and other places. Every five or six weeks I spent a Saturday and Sunday at Norwood, as the train journey was less than an hour. My parents were amazed at my rate of growth.

In the second week at Leatherhead, I started at my new school, with all necessities (and one or two luxuries) supplied by Lord Beaverbrook. He bought my first fountain pen, a superb instrument that served me till 1956, when my colleagues at Tate and Lyle gave me a 'Parker Duofold'. The Parker lasted me till the year 2000, so only two fountain pens had served me well for 60 years. Except in French and Latin, which I had never studied, I was well up to standard at my new school. Three years' French and Latin study served me well when I went to Mercers' School in 1942, until the year 1947. My Latin has lapsed, but I can still write accurate French sixty years after my last lesson. Sometimes I even write poetry in French. My schoolmates near Leatherhead were pleasant but different. They moved in a different world from me, with money and large homes, but I imbibed the confidence of their wider world. I also became adept at tests and examinations, valuable experience for one who would spend twenty years of life in full-time study. Natural sciences repelled me, because you cannot personalise them. My method with all other written exams was to choose which questions to answer, devote the first paragraph of each answer to rewriting the question, in my own terms, not adding or omitting any essential. That done, I then answered MY question very fully. I have always had large handwriting, and I covered impressive quantities of exam paper every time. In a three-hour exam I have sometimes made four visits for more paper.

I was aware that my favoured circumstances would not outlast the war. In fact, they changed halfway, in 1942 when I took the

London County Council eleven-plus exam. I found the exam absurdly easy, having time to study every question twice. I knew that I had done well, but not how well. I only found out when my parents began to have offers of places at famous schools such as Dulwich College, only a mile from my home, and Mercers' School, hundreds of years older than Dulwich College, and sited in Barnards' Inn (of Court) in Holborn, by London City. By far the better package was offered by Mercers' School, where I could have my place from September 1942. So my rural retreat would be only three years, three wonderful years. I needed to get my boat back into waters where I was in control. Waters where I was ahead of the tide, and not playing catch-up. Lord Beaverbrook's bounty had done wonders, but my schoolmates were headed for positions of authority. I was only interested in positions of autonomy. I knew that authority is a poisoned chalice. It makes you responsible for other people as well as yourself. Autonomy gives you freedom of choice and action.

Leatherhead had one more bounty to give me, and I could not even have guessed at the manner of that particular providence.

AND THE EMPTINESS THEREOF

Two new bright stars
Spear through the sky tonight
And as their burning
Rockets fall away,
A thousand million voices
Seem to say

The heavens declare
The glory of the State –
and the emptiness thereof.

A little boy
(Coloured, or just white trash?)
Lies on some sacking
In a desert shack,
And from his face
Shows every kind of lack

While the heavens declare
The glory of the State –
And the emptiness thereof.

An infant female
Dies in a Russian hut.
Attentive ears
Could hear her as she wailed.
All her short life
The hopeless harvest failed.

But the heavens declare
the glory of the State –
And the emptiness thereof.

BATTLE HYMN OF THE REPUBLICS

Good King Wenceslas
Looked out
While the people
Milled about
With a universal
Shout.
FREEDOM

Good King Wenceslas
Gave thanks
For the democratic
Ranks.
Suddenly he saw
Some tanks.
FREEDOM

Good Mayor Daley
Briefed his aides –
No assemblies
No parades
Nothing
Except gas grenades.
FREEDOM

Democrats
Of East and West
Know which policy
Pays best.
Heart of gold
In iron vest.
FREEDOM

5

Surprised By Joy

When C.S. Lewis experienced Christian conversion, he was 'surprised by joy', three words that became the title of his autobiography. Lewis, apart from his academic works, wrote two distinctly different types of books. He is famous for his allegorical fantasies, such as *The Lion, The Witch and The Wardrobe* (Narnia Books) and his series of three science fiction novels *Out of the Silent Planet, Perelandra* and *Voyage to Venus*. I am allergic to Science Fiction and to allegorical fantasy. They are diets too rich for digestion. They are sick making. J.R.R. Tolkien wrote titillation tripe and Mervyn Peake was a merchant of madness. There are dozens of others I could name, retailers of rabid rubbish, much of which gets filmed.

But C.S. Lewis wrote other, wonderful works such as *Mere Christianity, The Four Loves, The Screwtape Letters, The Great Divorce* and *Pilgrim's Regress*, among the best of their kind ever written. Lewis was a split personality, as his personal history reveals. His link with Leatherhead was that he did some studies there with George Macdonald which influenced the fantastic side of his work. Lewis's link with me is a mere three words, 'Surprised by Joy'.

In autumn 1940 my brother left Leatherhead to join the Home Office at Bournemouth. It was the start of his 44 years as a civil servant (his six years in the Royal Navy counted as Home Office years). John was 16 years of age, and I was nine years old. I was a very large nine-year old, at least two years bigger than my schoolmates. I never saw my schoolmates out of school hours. Morning and afternoon I rode my bicycle into and out of their privileged world. We only had classroom and dining room contact. It got me used to my habitual situation, all my life, of being 'extra to Establishment'. It has arisen time and time again during 70 years, being an inside 'outsider'. One of my favourite books is Colin Wilson's landmark first book *The Outsider*, a study of alienation in some people of genius.

In 1940, 1941 and 1942 all my social life, apart from my foster-parents, was with the age 12–14 year boys at my brother's secondary school, and with any local friends they had made. Most of those locals were girls who found Londoners livelier than the local boys. Most local boys disliked us. We were resented just as the American G.I.s who came to Britain in 1942, 1943 and 1944 were resented by adults. Much of that resentment was due to G.I. success with girls. One of the local girls who tagged along with us Londoners was a small, dark-haired, pretty girl called Joy. Her mother was a war widow, and Joy was her only child. Mother worked full time in a local factory, and had a busy social life every evening and weekend. Joy was very much left to her own devices, and she was the only local girl who attended much to me, perhaps because I was interested in her, and we had long conversations about our lonely situations.

All summer 1940 I had taken her, on the crossbar of my bike, to Box Hill, a high vantage point to observe the Battle of Britain in the air. The summer of 1940 had clear skies and drowsy heat, and we spent hours watching the aerial dogfights through battered old binoculars. By September 1940 the German air force had been forced to change their plans against Britain, and Box Hill was no longer a grandstand for hundreds of people to attend First Division War Matches. Joy was a war orphan, and we both agreed with Winston Churchill's assessment of our young RAF pilots, "Never in the history of human conflict has so much been owed by so many" (the whole free World) "to so few". I have recently contributed to a great memorial to those brave pilots in the heart of London.

In 1941 and 1942 one of the regular places of resort for our gang of about twenty boys and girls was Fetcham Splash. The village of Fetcham was the nearest to our part of Leatherhead, but it was on the other side of the River Mole, so named because it spends part of its distance underground. It was an average flowing waterway, dangerously reedy, but pleasant on a warm summer day. Ducks, and other waterfowl were there, and it was very little distance from where I lived. To take the risk of swimming at Fetcham Splash, especially when alone, I had two airfilled 5-gallon petrol cans linked by strong rope, and passed the rope under my back and armpits. A vigorous kickstroke could produce steady progress, but was quite tiring. The water was also very cold. My other travel in the River Mole was in a dug-out canoe, hacked with a hand-axe from a fallen tree. It floated well but I had to add outriggers for stability.

One day in spring 1942, about ten of us were halfway to Fetcham Splash, near some field hedges and a few trees. We were swinging on a single rope attached to the high bough of a tall tree. At the base of the rope was a strong footrest wide enough for two pairs of feet. The rope was a thick ship's rope that looked strong enough to last for ever. Best fun was for a girl to hold the rope and to stand on the footrest in the circle of a boy's arms. Others pushed the pair to a swinging arc. Around teatime all the others, except Joy and I, went home to eat. Joy had no set mealtimes, and my foster parents didn't dine until 7pm., so we had plenty of time. To try a showy venture, I climbed several feet up a dead tree, holding the rope and stick, and launched myself like Tarzan (but silently). At the end of the arc, the knot at the top of the rope broke from the bough, and I flew (with rope) into a high hedge of hawthorn. I was both roped and impaled, and I was losing blood. Joy was horrified, and set off for the farm to get help. Meanwhile, I had time to think. Every year that tree bore red fruit, with many uses, some of them medicinal. My blood was now staining the tree, and draining my veins. It was not what Nature intended.

Two men from the farm got me out of the tree, and taken away to hospital. Examination showed that I had no broken bones. Next day, I was relaxed in my hospital bed when Joy arrived to visit me. She was dressed in her best, and carried a folded topcoat. She pulled a chair close to the bed, rested her coat between us, and gave me a sisterly peck on the cheek. We chatted for a few minutes, until I felt my private parts being caressed. One of Joy's arms was burrowed beneath the bedding, below the coat. It was a planned operation. She had cracked Stalag Luft Hospital with a Trojan Coat. The tunnelling was secret, but my reaction was getting stronger. As it became uncontainable, she had a large cloth that prevented any sheet stains. She folded the cloth in on itself, and put it in the coat pocket. River Rubicon had been crossed. Friendly conversation became the whispers of lovers, warm words and promises of pleasures to come. When Joy left she gave me a splendidly UNsisterly kiss on the lips. A pulse reading at that time would have been very high. I was captive to love, or was it lust. Or was it both?

We met a few days later, and in the twenty weeks that remained of my time in Leatherhead we met two or three times a week to share sensual secrets. Three years older than me but much smaller, Joy was a perfect partner. Lord Beaverbrook had <u>bought</u> me an education; Joy was <u>giving</u> me one. Yet it was the clash of these two educations that took me away from Leatherhead, away from Joy, sooner than expected.

SHEPHERD'S WARNING

The morning sky was red – under the grey.
Bus, Bus, I said, Go mad. Bear me away
To sunshine. The Bus said, Town life is sweet,
And warned me: MIND YOUR HEAD WHEN LEAVING SEAT.

Seven more stops, Bus, and I shall be gone,
And then a winter-coated girl got on,
Opened her heavy coat, and changed my morning,
Facing me, underneath the Bus's Warning.

Perfect bare legs, still showing last year's tan,
Almost no skirt, and part of some great plan,
Firm bra-less breasts bursting a buttoned blouse.
I gazed as much as sanity allows.

And, at my stop (the sky was now less red)
Looked at the Warning, handed her my head,
Said, "You mind that, while I reserve my seat."
ALL PUBLIC NOTICES ARE INCOMPLETE.

THE PRODIGAL SON

Behold
A young man
With long hair
And a flowered Kaftan
Took his Study Grant
And went into
A far city.

And he took part
In Protests
And Sit Ins
And Referenda
And Direct Actions
Until all his substance
Was spent.

So he returned home
And said unto his father,
Father, I have sinned
Against Senate
And before thee,
And am no more worthy
To be called thy son.

And his father
Fell upon his neck
And broke it.

6

Kissing The Queen

In the middle months of 1942, I was living one dream down in Surrey, with my little lover Joy. At Norwood, my parents were living a different dream. They were receiving letters from headmasters of famous schools, offering me a place for five or seven years at their centuries-old academies. It was all due to my results in the London County Council Eleven Plus Examinations. When I took the exam, I was not aware of dropping any marks at all, and my impression must have been correct. Very wisely, my parents did not inform me until they had whittled the many school offers down to two. Those two schools merited visits and interviews during the summer months. The obvious one was Dulwich College only one mile from my Norwood home, and an easy walk for a Day Boy Scholar. Dulwich was an area that I had known for many years, the unique suburb, created around 1600 by friends and colleagues of William Shakespeare, as an investment of their theatrical wealth. The two theatrical names associated with Dulwich are Edward Alleyn (for the College and another school), and Richard Burbage (tragic actor) for one long road and property. Dulwich was also one of the favourite walks of William Blake (poet, engraver and visionary) where he used to see angels in the trees, and talk to the angels. In recent years, Prime Minister Margaret Thatcher bought a house at Dulwich, but never lived there. (I suspect that Denis Thatcher chose that house, because it is adjacent to a golf course.)

My parents' simple choice of school would have been Dulwich College, less than half an hour walk from the house where we lived. But my parents rarely obeyed the obvious. The interview with the Dulwich headmaster turned out to be a disaster. Finally, my mother led me out of his room, and out of the great gates, muttering, "the man's an idiot". Very soon after, we learned that he had to have psychiatric treatment, and eventually retire.

The school offers were now down to one, several miles away, on the edge of the City of London, at Holborn. Mercers' School (1170–1959) was nearly 500 years older than Dulwich College, and half the size, about 400 boys. During 800 years, the last of its many homes was Barnard's Inn (of Court), near Gray's Inn, Lincoln's Inn (of the eponymous fields) and the great legal centres from Chancery Lane through to the Strand. Barnard's Inn stands on the corner of Fetter Lane and Holborn, and it is now Gresham College, an adult College, endowed by Sir Thomas Gresham, the founder of the Royal Exchange. Gresham had been a scholar at Mercers' School in the 1500s, as had Sir Richard Whittington in the 1300s. He was Lord Mayor of London in 1397 and 1398, 1406 and 1407, and 1419/1420 (is that three times or six times?). Nowadays nobody serves more than one year! When Dick Whittington died in 1423, one of his many bequests was to rebuild a more comfortable Newgate Prison, a few hundred yards from where I went to school. On the opposite corner of Fetter Lane (from my school) was the hostelry where condemned prisoners from Newgate took their final refreshment before the long cart journey to Tyburn (Marble Arch) to be hanged. Rev. John Wesley, founder of Methodism, looked at those condemned men, and said, "There, but for the grace of God, go I". Another religious link with Fetter Lane is that the Moravian Church there saw the childhood worship by William Blake, which inspired him to his strange works of religion, including his many years of naked worship at home. I used to look at dull old Fetter Lane, and marvel!

The school was founded by a bequest of Thomas à Becket, the murdered Archbishop of Canterbury (also son of a Mercer) in 1170. His will was executed by his sister Agnes, whose head and shoulders appear on the school badge. The lady's coronet gives the impression that she was royal. Her sculpted image on the school wall is 'The Queen'. On a summer afternoon in 1942, my mother and I attended a meeting with the headmaster of Mercers' School, R. W. Jepson, author of two literary classics, *Clear Thinking* and *The Writer's Craft*. He welcomed us into his study, where we enjoyed tea and biscuits while we chatted generally. It was the end of the school day, and boys were walking past the study windows towards the Porter's Lodge and Holborn and home. The pupils lived at the four corners of London and beyond and few saw each other out of school hours. In my five years none of the other boys lived near Norwood. When the last boys had gone home, Mr. Jepson turned the conversation to what his school had to offer. My mother and I were well satisfied with the package, and agreed that I should start in September 1942.

There was much to be done, including going to Gorringe's Emporium in Buckingham Palace Road, to buy my school uniform, and various items of sports kit. Gorringes appears in a story about Queen Mary, wife of King George V. Visiting a little Kensington girl in hospital, the Queen asked, "Where do you live?". "Near Barkers," the girl replied. "That's interesting", said Queen Mary, "because I live near Gorringes." Our London preparations were quite easy, but the Leatherhead conclusions were more difficult. Arthur and Lilian, my foster-parents, were puzzled by my departure, as the war looked far from finished. Why was I going back into the bombs and the danger? Lilian even cried about it, and my mother hugged her. I promised them I would visit them once a month, a promise I kept for nearly twenty years. Most puzzled of all was Joy. We were very happy together, yet I was going to leave her for a fusty old school! She guessed that boys and girls have different priorities. I promised her that I would see her once a month, and kept that promise for about four years, until she married a soldier. My marvellous months with Joy did not invite reflection, but the breakaway needed to be rationalised. It is what I do. Everything needs to be rationalised. A poet's vocation is to take the particular and make it general, so I thought of my recent experience, and made a mental list:

Girls (and women?) can be as keen on sex as boys are.
Given the right conditions girls will make the first move.

If you don't start a relationship, or end it, then you have no responsibility except to be kind and pleasant.

Three thoughts in sequential order. I was under twelve years of age, and looking for long-term answers. For the next twelve years, until my twenty-fourth year, these thoughts served me well, and I had many happy relationships. What happened in my twenty-fourth year changed everything, and has stayed changed for fifty years. You will soon read all about it.

By September 1942 I was back in London, and ready for my new school, which started its academic year that month. Initially I travelled by tram from West Norwood to Holborn Subway, then walked along Holborn to the school gates. My journey time was an hour and a half, so I was spending three hours a day on travel. I used to do my homework on the evening tram home. Very soon I changed to train travel, from Gipsy Hill Station to Holborn Viaduct Station, and my travel became only two hours a day.

On the day I started secondary school, I was shiny and new, in creaky black shoes, grey long trousers, black blazer with silver badge, black cap with silver badge, grey shirt and claret and gold tie. My large brief case was brown leather, and it served me well for five school years, and nine years at Tate and Lyle. At the school gates I followed other boys past the porter's lodge, and past the narrow entry into the area in front of the head's study. Boys were everywhere but the new ones were conspicuously not in the noisy chattering groups. High on the wall was the sculpture of the lady on the school badge, not royal, but in school jargon 'The Queen'. The one rite of passage for a new boy was to 'Kiss The Queen', by climbing up a ladder of boys' backs and pressing one's face to the effigy. After that I was a Mercers' schoolboy.

Although the school was a good place to be, I always question everything around me. From the outset I would not want to remain involved in anything that seemed irrelevant. Pupils are always under tutorial judgement. Tutors are always under judgement by pupils. I was doubtful about science, because all sciences are dead religions. I had to discover how the science teachers of Mercers' School promoted dead religions. By my second year I had realised that I was NOT interested in science, so I quietly dropped out of sciences, to nobody's regret. The Biology master, Dr. Whitehouse, lived in another world. His only requirement of a boy was to carry a sharp knife to dissect passing frogs. The Physics master I never registered. I think he disappeared into a prism, and came out as fragments of many colours. The King of the Chemistry lab was a charismatic character E.G. "Eggy" Andrews. I was too charismatic for his liking, so we parted on smiling terms. I had also bowled him out first ball at cricket.

The Mathematics master, Mr. Fison, must have been a genius, for he got me to Distinction level in a subject (or three subjects if you include algebra and geometry) that I did not really enjoy. He had an earlier career in Ordnance Survey. Another man of maps was Mr. Devereux, the Geography master, whose own publications were used for many of his lessons. He interested me in his subject. History also had a good teacher, G.G. Allen, a large man with a large mind. He was also a competent musician on the double bass. The Latin master, Mr. Scott, was pleased to find that I had three years experience of the language, and I managed to maintain a good standard and enjoy Latin literature. I do not remember the name of the art master, but I valued his keen interest in calligraphy. My handwriting improved, and I enjoyed several aspects of Art, design and colour. In the same building as art was the man of Music (was he Doctor?) Rowsell, composer of the School Song, and very interested in folk music and English songs. I enjoyed singing, but my only musical instrument is the harmonica. Still in the same building, a demon wrestler called McKenzie pushed us through physical education. I did just enough to get by, as a gymnasium is a place I would normally avoid.

Two teachers I would never avoid were Stuart Moss, who taught French, and Vernon Rossetti, the young English teacher. Stuart Moss had a golden touch with French. He also had an attractive French wife. They were the embodiment of the Entente

Cordiale! After three years of basic French studies, at a private school near Leatherhead, I was ready for much more French. Stuart Moss gave it, and his teaching has enriched my life. How much we owe to a really gifted teacher. Equally brilliant was Vernon Rossetti, who enthused me for Shakespeare, and many other aspects of English Literature. He introduced me to the plays of George Bernard Shaw, and he produced *St. Joan* at the school. It was my gateway to the delights of drama, which has given me sixty years of pleasure. I hope that my decades of teaching English Literature have given as much pleasure.

Twice a week I was involved with soccer or cricket, or cross-country running. I always stayed on the comfort side of effort, but I managed to win Second Eleven Cricket Colours and a handsome red blazer with gold badge.

The school sports field was at Grove Park, South London, many miles from the school, and the long trek twice a week was annoying. One Wednesday, from the train out of London Bridge to Grove Park, I saw the Surrey Docks ablaze, from a daylight raid by German bombers. The only other two war incidents associated with school that I remember were climbing over the piled rubble of Prudential Insurance Headquarters in Holborn while walking to school, and, in 1944, one of the first V2 rockets fell on Smithfield Market, and shook the school with its vast explosion. In autumn 1944, due to the V2 Rockets, I missed a whole term of school, from September to Christmas, because I was sent to stay with my grandparents at York. I spent ten weeks working for my great-uncle Percy Benson at his Little Salt Factory in Bedern, an historic courtyard near York Minster. Because of the war, all his employees were teenage girls, and I was given a warm welcome by those lively lasses of York. Being a true patriot, I lay back and thought of England. Perhaps keeping girls happy was my War Effort? I was still only thirteen years of age.

Also in 1944, my father's cousin, Group Captain 'Percy' Pickard ('F. for Freddy' in the bomber film *Target for Tonight*) was sent on a special mission to Amiens in Picardie, France. At dawn

45

light on 18th February 1944, with a Group of Mosquito fighter-bombers, he flew to Amiens gaol and blew the walls apart, to allow hundreds of prisoners to escape from the Nazis. Some of the prisoners knew some of the plan for D–Day (still four months ahead) and if the Gestapo had been able to apply torture, the whole Normandy Invasion might have been compromised, and the war lost. Group Captain Pickard died on that mission but saved the secrets of D–Day. He is buried at Amiens where his final heroism was shown. His brother (also Group Captain Pickard) was Commandant of R.A.F. Lyneham, Wiltshire, the great transport aerodrome.

I had two close escapes from death in the war. Late one night I was standing in the dark outside an air raid shelter, wearing the steel helmet my parents bought me, when a large piece of shell shrapnel fell two miles out of the sky, and knocked me to my knees in the gutter. The gash in my helmet shows it would have split my head in two, killing me instantly. The other incident was very strange. Early in 1944, Norwood was one of the heaviest sufferers from V1 (pilotless) Flying Bombs, propelled by a flame-jet. Our back garden was at the crest of a hill, and our Anderson shelter stuck up over that crest. Our shelter was covered with a yard of earth, and a thick jungle of nasturtiums. One night a V1 passed low over our shelter, while we covered our ears and trembled inside. Later, in the cold light of dawn, we found that the nasturtiums had been scorched by the Flying Bomb's jet. Frightening. During 1940–1945 we lost all our house windows several times and lost our roof twice. Only fifty yards away, in Gibbs Square, a house like ours disappeared to dust, by a direct bomb hit.

After I returned from York at Christmas 1944 I had no difficulty picking up the threads of my studies, and, in 1946, I took many subjects in London University School Certificate. I obtained enough satisfactory results to get a London University Matriculation Certificate, which would prove valuable in 1947 and even more valuable in 1956. Priceless.

ESCAPIST

Why, if you feel like that, do you hang on
What more to say after what you have said?
Have you an honest longing to be gone,
Or are they simply sounds from out your head?

Would not a desert island suit your case,
Free from frustration, warmed by ceaseless sun?
Or would you not be happy any place,
Doleful in chains, doubtful where there are none?

Yes, that shells up your problem in a nut;
Without frustration as the oyster's grain
You'd sit outside your little wooden hut
And wish you were at loggerheads again.

When you had no just reason for complaint,
No irritant round which to grow your pearls,
No wild neurotic urge to write or paint,
You would be more vile-tempered than the churls.

No. Best remain among the din and smoke,
The slobs that prosper, and the saints that fall.
Then you can always have your little joke –
That you are longing to escape it all.

TIMEKEEPING

When I set out on any enterprise,
I must (as if all poetry should rhyme,
And scansion renders it the more sublime)
I must be sure my parts are all in time,
That all my little watches synchronise.

Though this may sound simplicity itself,
The sad reverse is very often true,
My heart may stand at twenty-five past two,
My head at three, my hands at quarter to,
And none be near the clock upon the shelf.

So, painful though the process has become,
I make adjustments here, advancements there,
Until my head, my hands, my heart, my pair
Of feet are all in time, and I'm aware
My soul is cramped, and slowly going numb.

All this can be so badly misconstrued
That when I'm gone, I wouldn't be surprised
If many said, the praise that he most prized
Was this, His little watches synchronised.
My ghost will not doubt answer something rude.

7

Out Of The Strong (Came Forth Sweetness)

If you look on a tin of Lyle's Golden Syrup, you will find a picture of a lion, a swarm of bees and an Old Testament verse, "out of the strong came forth sweetness", (Judges 14.14), a riddle set by Samson. In the decade up to 1956, I had plenty of Sweetness from Tate and Lyle, and this is how it happened.

During Autumn 1946 my father told a Tate and Lyle manager that I had passed my London University matriculation, and I would be interested in City employment. Father had deduced that I was not happy at school, because much at Mercers' School had changed. The departure of one man, and the arrival of another had made the difference. Mr. Jepson had gone and William Haden was the new Headmaster. Haden had been an Army Officer for several years, and he could not forget it, nor let anyone else forget it. He even got Field-Marshal Montgomery to visit the school for a pep-talk. Like the British voters in 1945, I was not in the mood to be regimented. Bill Haden even wanted me to start German studies. Perhaps he admired their military precision? Mr. Jepson had never ordered me to do anything. He had even let me give up all Sciences. He trusted my judgement. The German teacher was very coercive, so I lampooned him as 'Mr. Vee Haf Vays of Making you Study German'. Some of my satirical verse had already been published. The German teacher and Bill Haden were not happy. The time had come for a parting of the ways.

Suddenly I had a life-changing invitation. The Tate and Lyle manager made my father aware that there was a junior vacancy in the accounts department. I had a (totally unexpected) distinction in mathematics. I was offered the vacancy by Tate and Lyle, and it was arranged I should start after Easter 1947. The slight delay was very helpful, as Britain was suffering its most bitter, brutal winter in living memory. Month after month, until March 1947, saw more and more snow and ice. Travel was terrible. I was in the Lower VI Form, but my studies were not going anywhere, and I did not travel to school if the weather was worse on any particular day. By March 1947 I had said all my form farewells. All that remained was to thank my favourite schoolmasters, to empty my desk, and to walk out of the big gates for the last time. I made a vow that, if I lived fifty more years, I would join the Old Mercers' Club. In summer 1997 (50$1/2$ years on) I joined the club, and have found it worthwhile. Michael Jepson, the son of my first Mercers headmaster, asked me, in 2004, to write a verse history of the Old Mercers' Club, in fewer than fifty lines. At the centenary luncheon (April 2004) in the magnificent Mercers' Hall, in the City of London, I realised that it was exactly 57 years since I had left the school. The school closed (for ever) in 1959, after 789 years. Despite the closure, the Mercers' Company still spend millions of pounds each year on education. My 48 lines on the history of the Old Mercers' Club have gone to all members and interested persons worldwide. When I walked out of Barnard's Inn building in 1947, I was aware that my life had been accelerated, as in 1942 and in 1939. More Poet Luck. It seemed that I had bypassed graduate studies. What no-one knew was that I would have ten years of full-time study for three different graduate qualifications, in my twenties, my thirties and my forties.

In April 1947 I started in the accounts office of Tate and Lyle, in its wartime 'exile' address, 52 Cadogan Square, the former residence of De La Rue, the playing card and printing millionaire. It was an amazing building, unlike any other office I have encountered. Playing cards are in packs of 52, suites of 13. Some features of the décor were 13, 26 or 52. I never counted the vertical lift mirrors, but a lone lift user felt surrounded by a small crowd. All offices were adapted from house rooms, and the house confirmed the feeling of one big happy family. They were the most paternal and indulgent employers I have ever seen. I was told that very few people had ever voluntarily left their employ. I can well believe it. Why would one leave happy, highly paid heaven? But I did.

The accounts office had only six staff, including myself and the boss William Gowing. Very few for financial focus of a national and international company. The only machine in the accounts department was a BRUNSVIGA calculator operated by hand, and very small in size. The other high technology was a rubber stamp with every possible variant of the company name, for endorsing the backs of cheques. In that almost Dickensian office, I started at 9.30am, as we were still (two years after the war) working 'wartime hours'. That was because the enforced move from the City had made most people's journey to work longer and slower. All my colleagues were eccentric, in varying degrees. (Can it be that I was the only normal one?) Charles Cosgrove Paternoster, wielder of the rubber stamp, received millions of pounds of cheques each week, and processed them for paying in at the bank. Banks then closed at 3pm., so at 2.30pm a smart commissionaire with a lockable briefcase collected the day's cheques, and walked to the bank. For a few weeks I accompanied him to learn the procedure, and to meet the bank staff. One day we were late, and saw the bank doors closed. I climbed in the transom window in a back alley and delivered the cheques to startled staff. It was a bad scare, as we wondered about a day's interest on possibly half a million pounds! We were never late again.

C.C. Paternoster was so lanky, languid and elegant that his tailoring and his accent were worthy of Jeeves or Bertie Wooster. The oldest man in Accounts was actually called Bertie. He was a charming chap from Amersham (I was always amazed how far people travelled to the office). Bertie had fought in World War One, and was full of small shrapnel too dangerous to remove. He was very much alive 29 years after that war, and was an officer in the St. John Ambulance Brigade. The other two were only ten years older than I was, and had served in World War Two. One was a fiery ginger-haired man, who used to spend his lunch hour power-walking round Chelsea, getting thin and fit. The other was very precise, and used a sign-writer's mahl-stick for every letter and figure he wrote. Perfect precision on every page. Our boss,

Bill Gowing, was the oddest of all. He was rosy-faced, short and fat, and always wore a black jacket with striped morning trousers, looking like he had stepped out of an Austin Reed advertisement. He told us of his social success (like Pooter in *Diary of a Nobody*) at Reading, Tilehurst and Pangbourne, where he lived. He and his wife had more social strategems than 'Norman' (of the fish knives) in John Betjeman's poem about social status. When not describing their latest social triumph, he went out to other offices for long periods. In our office, we never saw him do anything but keep the safe keys and the cash box, and look at work that we had done for him.

The petty cash box was under constant demand by directors and managers for cashing cheques from Monday to Friday. On Saturdays no directors, managers or senior staff attended, so 'Ginger', Mahl-Stick and I (one each week) kept a three-week rota of Saturdays, when we alone held the vital keys. One director lived in the house at Cadogan Square, in the penthouse flat, above all the offices. He was Sir George Vernon Tate, and he and Lady Tate had a delightful daughter, Virginia, who lived with them. The only raider of the cash box on Saturday mornings was Sir George, who cashed cheques for £100 or £200. One Saturday he cashed a cheque for £400, which almost defeated the petty cash. His world-weary explanation was "My wife is giving a party". Four hundred pounds was almost my annual salary. Sir George always chatted for half an hour, and I learned of his boyhood in the City (possibly more menial than mine) when he ran business errands in all directions as "apprenticeship". My father worked in Seething Lane only one hundred yards from the company's City offices, and I had spent scores of Saturday mornings and occasional Sundays with my father, exploring the area, so I was able to discuss with Sir George the ways through the City. I also told him that I had met, at my father's office, a young man called James Callaghan (Inland Revenue Staff Federation, who later became a Member of Parliament, Prime Minister and First Lord of the Treasury). Sir George was keen on the arts, and knew Picasso, as befits a descendant of the founder of the Tate Gallery.

When he learned that I was publishing a volume of verse called *City Pages*, and that my £100 would produce 500 copies, he said he knew many who would be interested in a book of verse about the City. He promptly doubled my stake with a £100 cheque of his own, and reserved 200 copies of the book. Thanks to his help, I was able to publish 1,000 copies of *City Pages*, and Sir George eventually bought far more than his original 200 copies. I know that one book went to Sir J. Arthur Rank (later Lord Rank) of Rank, Hovis, McDougall, who was also the king of British films. Sir George also gave copies to all the Tates and Lyles in Head Office, about ten people, including Lord Lyle of Westbourne, Alex Lyle and Sir Ian Lyle and 'Tony' Tate who shared an office with Tom Marshall, the Company Secretary. One Christmas I found the pair of them on their knees with a large trainset. They were not in the least abashed. They took my information, and played on. Two other boosts for my first book were bonuses. When I paid in Sir George's personal cheque to my bank account I became a 'V.I.P.' with the bank. I later sold several copies there. Even more pleasant was when I joined the Poetry Society, I met the new editor of *Poetry Review*, Muriel Spark, later famous for short stories and twenty two novels. She was more feisty than her (The Prime Of) Miss Jean Brodie, and I was her toy boy for two years, until I joined the Army for National Service. Muriel liked my first book, and even gave a few to her friends. She went to live in New York and later to Italy, but we corresponded regularly for about ten years. She became a keen Roman Catholic in 1954, the year that I became a keen Anglican. After that she called me her heretical friend, but surely I was only schismatic?

My first book *City Pages* eventually sold 2,000 copies (by age 18) and funded my next book. I have always funded my books from the previous ones, and I was soon able to produce 5,000 copies per book, which took a few years to sell. In recent years (1976 to 2006) one of my books has sold 60,000 copies (12 editions of 5,000) but it took 30 years to do so. My first 2,000 books were also useful as 'visiting cards', and enriched my social life up to

1951, when I published my second book *Punch Lines*, verses of Satire, Parody and mock-Chaucer. It had a spin-off, in the form of a 32-page mock-Chaucer booklet about 'Sir Claude of Southwarke', "who was a very perfit gentil Knighte (excepting always when that he was tyte"). 'Sir Claude' was popular until my third book BRISTOLIANA in 1957 at Bristol. The sweetest 'sweetness' that emerged from my first two years at Tate and Lyle was also helped by my first book.

When some colleagues lunched at a pub called 'The Australian', and 'Ginger' power-walked around Chelsea, I went to the 'British Restaurant' in Cadogan Gardens, plain food at plain prices. Most of my fellow lunchers were women, many self-employed and locally resident. Three of them remained my friends for several years. One in particular, a tall elegant translator (in Scandinavian languages) used to give me tea and sympathy after my working day. She even translated some of my poems into forms that could be used in education, and sold them in Scandinavia for school publications. We were close friends until she went back to Scandinavia in 1954.

From 1947 to 1949 I worked at 52 Cadogan Square, the first two of my Tate and Lyle years, before I did two years National Service in the Army. I was well in at the Poetry Society, writing many poems and my first hundred commissioned works (mostly sonnets) based on detailed information by the purchaser. All the early sonnets cost £5 (for 14 lines). After February 1971 (decimal currency) I charged £10, and nowadays £20 (still only £1.43 per line, a bargain). Muriel Spark took me to some of the places which later appeared in her novels. The women's hostel in *Girls of Slender Means* was clear. Muriel and I were both interested in Gerard Manley Hopkins' "The Wreck Of The Deutschland" (a ship that sank) but I never met the girl who died (in *Girls of Slender Means*) while reciting that poem in a burning building. Maybe I did meet her, without knowing? I certainly did meet Muriel's two other boyfriends, the noted author Derek Stanford (her academic boyfriend), and Howard Sergeant (her ballroom

54

dancing boyfriend) who was the founder and Editor of OUTPOSTS poetry magazine from 1944, of which I have all 180 editions. Howard and I became good friends, and corresponded until he died. 1947 to 1949 also introduced me to the drama group and social life of the headquarters of the Young Women's Christian Association, Queen Mary Hall, Great Russell Street. The women at Queen Mary Hall played a major part in my life until 1956, and I still write to two of them. I also formed friendships with some British Overseas Airways stewardesses who lived at Chelsea Cloisters. I also had friends at the Institut Français, Kensington, and some in Pimlico, near where Anthony Armstrong-Jones had his photographic studio. The late 1940s and early 1950s still influence my life, more than fifty years on, because those years were full of Poet Luck.

THERE'S NO FUSCHIA IN IT

A garden is a lovesome thing, God wot
A lot of work it takes and what
A lot of dirt it makes
To tramp about the house.

A garden is a place where bees may buzz
And swarm, and when it's warm one does
Nothing
Unless one aster.

A garden is a place where one may plant
Bulbs, though for the life of me I can't
Think why I planted hyacinths.
They've grown no hyacinths I last looked.

A garden is a place where things may grow
Apace, if only one is really in the know
How to apply phosphates and nitrates
At the right rates.

A garden may imbue you with an urge
To cultivate until you're on the verge
Of breakdown, and you say, "I quite forgot
A garden is a lovesome thing God wot."

FULFILMENT

I built a patio
In my backyard

And waited till a day
Of streaming sun

Then sat there sipping
Long drinks laced with rum

Wishing, I swear,
Nobody any ill

Yet feeling all the while
Licensed to kill.

When skies are grey
And other things are hard

I touch the patio
In my backyard.

SNOWSHOES

Looking for something else
I found my snowshoes,
And I remember bitter
Struggles in them, long ago.

How long since anything
Was a struggle, anything
Was an effort? God,
I am surely not wanting snow?

8

Wheels Within Wheels

Saints have a passion for God. In the tenth chapter of the book of Ezekiel, in the Old Testament, "wheels within wheels" is a picture of God. In Ezekiel 10.13, the prophet says, "as for the wheels, they were called, in my hearing, the whirling wheels". Early evidence of the divinity of cycling. If one is not a saint, and if one avoids passion in human relationships, it has to break out somewhere else. In my case it made three outbreaks – poetry, books and bicycles. From primary school to the present day poetry has fuelled my fire, and the same years have seen my personal library grow to 11,000 books and shrink back to 7,000 books, many of which I hope to sell soon.

But my driving, drooling passion for seventy years has been bicycles, not always cycling, but bicycles, which are pedal wheels attached to chain wheels, linked to hub wheels attached to road wheels, all in a whirling dance. In all Europe, in all Britain, in city, town or village, I cannot pass a bicycle shop. I window-gaze, I go in and ask technical questions, I buy things for which I have no immediate use. No drug addict is more addicted. No gambler is more hooked. On a steam-train day outing to Watchet in Somerset, I saw a bike-shop on its final day before closure. I spent over an hour and over a hundred pounds on rare spare bicycle parts, which kept me happy for years. Some I sold on, and made other 'nutters' happy. Alexander von Tutschek, a friend of mine at Bath, reconstructed his house to have more room for bicycles. He is a splendidly manic man, as all of us members of the Veteran Cycle Club are. But is not only a veteran thing. Before I was nine years old, I had four cycles. Now that I am approaching 80 years, I have an exercise bicycle, an elegant tricycle, two racing bikes, two touring bikes and a shed full of spares. No sandboy is happier than barmy Bill. From age sixteen to date, I have had another fifteen racing, touring, or all-terrain bikes, some of them handbuilt to my instructions. I also had an upright bicycle polo bike, but I got badly bruised by mallets aforethought, so I quickly gave up bicycle polo. My most special bike was a handbuilt grass-track machine, with bamboo wheel-rims and stainless steel spokes, tied and soldered at every crossing. On a flat grass track, every corner is a centrifugal crisis to be fought and beaten. Between 1947 and 1956 I had great fun on grass tracks. Those ten years, (before I went to Bristol) were my most active in the Kentish Wheelers, an all-male club founded in 1903, the same year as the first Tour de France. Our badge was the White Horse of Kent. We had a racing cabin at Herne Hill Stadium. We had a country headquarters for time-trial weekends. When I joined, after World War Two, our President was W.F. 'Sandy' Holdsworth, maker of Holdsworth bicycles, who had professional racing teams, home and abroad. His brother Jack was also prominent, and the brothers held many tandem records between the wars. Tandems had a large place in K.W. Club history, and the last managers of tandem-paced solo racing were Jack Killingback and Bill Mumford, experts at an event long since gone. We had several star track riders, and a few fine time trialists on the roads, including champion teams, and one Road Record holder for London to Brighton and back, A.R.J. (Alf) Hill the pedalling postman, who did that difficult ride in 4 hours, 32 minutes 19 seconds, a two minute beating of Ken Joy's time. Three years later Ken Joy reduced Alf's record by seven minutes, an awesome achievement. It was not beaten again for seventeen more years.

When I did my two 'end to end' rides in 1952 and 1953, I only did them as a tourist, taking 10 days for the 900 miles, with no planning or preparation. In 1952, in honour of the Queen's accession, I rode from Land's End to John O'Groats. In 1953, in honour of the Queen's Coronation, I rode from John O'Groats to Land's End, all alone. They remain two of the great experiences of my life. Other great experiences in cycling were in 1948. The first open time trial of the season was the Kentish Wheelers

Novices 25 Miles, and I was Number 1, so I started the whole road time trials Season. My event place was only about 50th fastest, but a Kentish Wheeler did win the event, the younger of the two Roth brothers. I was a moderate racer, because I never approached the pain barrier, but my times were so variable that I presented problems for handicappers, and could sometimes beat them and win a handicap prize. King of the handicappers was Frank Fischer, founder of the 300,000 Mile Club for long-distance cyclists. In the past fifty years, individual total distance records have gone beyond 400,000 miles, past half a million, past 600,000 miles and 700,000 miles. A select few are beyond 800,000 miles and one has hopes of reaching One Million Miles. Maybe.

My other special experience of 1948 was being a competitors' steward at Herne Hill for the London Olympic Games. I owed that to two very influential people, Reg Harris, supreme sprinter who won two Olympic Medals, and Charles King OBE, our Club chairman, who was also Legal Clerk to Lord Denning, the Master of the Rolls. In summer 1948 I spent a month with the track cyclists of all the world (speaking my fairly good French) and obtaining all their day-to-day requirements. For that I received a full set of free tickets. Tate & Lyle gave me a month's extra leave to do it.

I regarded all my racing activities as fun. Part of that fun was to find crafty, small grass track meetings in the country, and have a rural weekend with a busy Saturday and a relaxed Sunday. Two or three friends and a van were helpful to get to remote locations. One could sometimes fit a Saturday track meet and a Sunday road time trial in one weekend. I was such a slacker that it took me eight years to get my 25-mile time under one hour, and never better than 59 minutes and 25 seconds. I never got my 50-mile time under 2 hours 3 minutes. My only hundred-mile race was outside 4 hours 10 minutes.

The only two hard tracks other than Herne Hill that I experienced were very shallow ones, with cornering problems. They were at Palmer Park, Reading and Preston Park, Brighton.

Those meetings usually combined running, field events and cycling, and I used to meet some fine athletes such as E. Macdonald Bailey, the 'Black Flash' of sprint running, and Gordon (Puff-Puff) Pirie, world-class distance runner. His nickname came from a breathing technique that inflated his cheeks. It obviously worked, as he held several world running records. In winter, I sometimes ran cross country practice at the training HQ of South London Harriers. We ran over Farthing Down, South of Croydon. Gordon Pirie emigrated to New Zealand, as a fitness trainer, but he died quite young. In tourist cycling, I visited every county of mainland Britain, plus the Isle of Wight and the Isle of Man. I have never been to Ireland. On the Isle of Man, I took twice as long as the racers to ride the 37³/4 miles circuit used by both cyclists and motor cyclists. But the thrill of free wheeling down from the mountain to Governor's Bridge and the finish was still a hair-raising experience.

I was once privileged to meet the greatest cyclist ever, Beryl Burton of Morley, Leeds. She was for 25 consecutive years the time-trial best all-rounder averaged over 100 miles, 50 miles, and 25 miles, every year from 1958 to 1982. Twenty-five consecutive years. I know of no other sport where that has been achieved. It amounts to a quarter century of total domination. But that was only one aspect of her achievements. Beryl Burton also won world track pursuit champion five times, and was British nation champion thirteen times. She was world road race champion twice, and second once. She was British national road race champion twelve times. In time trials she was national champion 100 miles eighteen times, national champion 50 miles twenty-three times, 25 mile champion 25 times, and 10 mile champion four times. She was Yorkshire Best All Rounder 25 times. The above tally totals seven world gold medals, four world silvers and four world bronze medals. One woman, 15 world championship medals.

Nationally, Beryl Burton won a total of 95 gold medals on the road and six silver medals, 101 total. She also won twenty-five gold best all rounder Yorkshire medals, every year of her record career. In 1967 she became the ONLY woman to beat a man's competition record, riding 277.25 miles in 12 hours. She was also the first woman to beat one hour for twenty-five miles, first under two hours for 50 miles, and the only woman to beat four hours for 100 miles.

Perhaps most amazing of all in 1968, Beryl was invited by the world's greatest PROFESSIONAL time trial, the 'Grand Prix des Nations', to compete over 73.5 kilometres (46 miles) against all the greatest male time triallists. The French had calculated that she would not average 40 kilometres per hour but she averaged almost 42kph., and found the end stadium totally unprepared for her. She had to burst through a track race to get to the line. She then had to ride two laps in the stadium. But the time keepers were not then ready! So she had to ride an extra lap for the convenience of the time keepers. She rode further than any of the MALE PROFESSIONALS! She averaged 41.853kph. She was 31 years of age, and the whole cycling world was stunned by her performance. She was an amateur who never had a trainer, nor any of the back-up of the Continental professionals. She had all the duties of a housewife and mother. She had an ordinary job in fruit farming, and refused professional contracts. She remembered the French spectators shouting "Allez, la Britannique". One French writer wrote, "If Beryl Burton had been French, Joan of Arc would have to take second place".

Her husband, Charlie Burton (who first introduced her to cycling) devoted about 30 years to Beryl's racing career, went to all of her events, home and abroad, and shares in her totally unbeatable career. I admire the great male riders, Armstrong, Indurain, Hinault, Merckx, Anquetil (five or more Tour de France wins each) but they have teams of road slaves to serve them. Beryl rode alone and totally unaided on the road. I admire the Welsh woman Nicole Cooke, now first in the world, but can she keep it up for twenty more years, till she is past forty years of age? No, only Beryl did that. She died at 58 years of age, while out cycling.

INTERNAL MEMORANDUM

"I just want him," she said. I wonder what
She meant by that, and where the stress is placed,
On "just" or "him"? A man could well have said
"I just want her," and then the listener
Would have the self-same problem – to infer
How, why and when, how long, how close, what for?

The statement drifts away into thin air.
The note of resignation, or despair,
Is usually present. But I ask
Cannot the speaker solve the simple task
Of first knowing oneself, and there can then
Be no false starting-point, ever again.

You're the complaint, so you must be detective;
(All counsel should be strictly non-directive).
You are the true and unique launching-place
Of anything you seek to send to Space.
Be sure, before you find the venture lost,
You know the target, and could pay the cost.

And if you could, can you still be sure,
That what rates now will rate for evermore?
To have and hold, to "live with" (without strings)
May look alike, but are two different things.
Contracts contract, while debts and doubts expand,
And time erodes not only dusty land.

If you must choose, and when you make your choice,
Be sure it is your unique inner voice
That says, "I will", and know how long, how close
You wish to be with whom you chose.
Better the stringless fling that leaves no scars
Than years of youth spent sighing for the stars.

THE LONG WALK

On the long walk
From Aldermaston to London
I saw a stranger
Walking with a limp,
Dragging a blistered foot.

He sat aside to rest.
But when I went to help
The man beside me said,
"He is a Russian." In
Such a tone of voice.

He is a spy. He is
A dirty dog. He is
Not one of us. Even
His blister is a
Fiendish subterfuge.

His blister was most real.
So was his gratitude.
Pain knows no language bar;
Plasters no politics.
Smiling, we journeyed on.

But not two strangers.
Just two weary men
Going the same way
For the same reason
On the long walk.

9

The Good Soldier Pick

Rudyard Kipling is usually credited with turning public attention away from generals and officers, and toward the common soldier. He is regarded as the champion of the other ranks, and he was. Some foreign authors have a cynical or humorous view of soldiers, and one such classic is *The Good Soldier Schweik*, which comes nearer to my experience.

Early in 1949 I was notified of my obligation to do National Service for a period of up to two years in the army. I was summoned to a medical examination at Hither Green in south London. After that, I was given my marching orders. One bright morning in July 1949, when I was eighteen years old, I reported to Parsons Barracks, Aldershot, Hampshire, the Basic Training Unit of the Royal Army Ordnance Corps. I was issued with a lot of khaki clothing and equipment, and for the next two years I was a defender of the realm, a soldier of King George VI. After two weeks intensive training in the elements of soldiering, I was posted to Wellington Lines, an old row of three barracks, well over a hundred years old, for a further ten weeks of training. The barrack blocks were named after three of the Duke of Wellington's battles in the Peninsular Campaign in Spain and Portugal, against the French. The battles were Salamanca, Talavera and Badajos. There was also a fairly new medical centre, a large officers' mess building, and a big parade ground.

Wellington Lines was a self-contained small world, and for ten weeks it was my home. Fortunately, it was summertime, because I shudder to think what the huge bleak rooms would have been like in winter. The stairs and iron balconies echoed to the sound of army boots. I was in Salamanca Barracks, named after a Spanish city about a hundred miles north of Madrid. The Iron Duke had a victory against the French at Salamanca in 1812, while Napoleon was leading another army across Russia to Moscow. Napoleon's army also suffered a great disaster that year. For food purposes, our mess hall was in the ground floor of our own block, quick and convenient at breakfast, lunch and dinner times. The food was good and plentiful, and I was always hungry. I do not remember any of my fifteen room companions from Salamanca, as everything was so large and impersonal. Even in easier environments I feel the need to personalise life.

While at Parsons Barracks I had fallen down a flight of concrete steps and damaged one ankle. It was strongly strapped during my time at Aldershot, and I was excused from wearing boots. It was a useful precedent, as 'excused boots' meant no marching. While all the others were square bashing in the large parade ground, I was given light duties in the company office. I was allowed to wear my highly polished, dark brown shoes, with no lace in the shoe on the injured foot. The medical officer was a young National Service man in his later twenties, new to army life. So new that he sometimes knocked his hat off when he saluted with his cane in hand. He was sympathetic about my injury. My only fatigue duties for ten weeks were officer's mess duties, doing mountains of washing up every evening. The bonus was that there were always a few top quality dinners left over, so I got a fourth cooked meal every day, and filled out my large bony body. Also, I never spent any of my money at Aldershot's entertainments. I used the money to buy quality khaki shirts and ties which I wore throughout my two years. I also bought two quality berets, and several spare badges and buckles. Having no parade obligations I could lend or rent my polished boots and brassware to any in urgent need of them, usually the recruits striving to become officers.

My twelve weeks at Aldershot flew by. In September and October I was under some pressure from the training officers to consider Intelligence Corps or officer training. My Intelligence Quotient was 168 (one higher than Carol Vorderman, of current fame on 'Countdown'). I was found unsuitable for Intelligence

Corps, and I signed a form 'Non-Desirous War Office Selection Board' – I opted out of officer training. The next choice in the Ordnance Corps for high I.Q. recruits was the ammunition examiner course at the Army School of Ammunition, at Bramley, Hampshire, halfway between Reading and Basingstoke. It was a huge ammunition depot, miles away from civilian populations. The whole Depot was 28 Battalion, R.A.O.C., of which 'B' Company was the School of Ammunition. The course took six months and was very intensive, so a photographic memory was helpful.

The battalion colonel was the famous Colonel Gore, wartime hero of Tobruk in North Africa, who was the temporary Commandant while awaiting Court Martial for doubtful deeds in Palestine before the state of Israel ever existed. 'B' Company never saw him, but we heard his huge Fraser-Nash sports car roaring around the roads at all hours of the day and night. He had at least two exotic girlfriends, and much social life in Reading. The Commandant of the School of Ammunition was Major Thompson, a brilliant technical officer who was also an acute manager of men. He could assess a man's job suitability with a month or two of observing a soldier on the course. It was largely to his credit that square pegs found square holes, and the round pegs found round ones at the varied depots all over Britain. The plum posting was Hyde Park Magazine, not a publication, but an ammunition depot in London's West End. The bright boys were sent near to the bright lights.

Major Thompson's private passion was amateur dramatics, and the 'Bramley Seedlings' were a talented group of thespians who produced several shows a year, including a pantomime which was a great annual event. To be in the 'Bramley Seedlings' was better fun than spending time and money in Reading or in Basingstoke. The drama company enhanced the army reputation in our part of Hampshire. When the full company took a pantomime to an outside location, it was a five-lorry convoy. There was a camp theatre, and two or three surplus Barrack rooms full of properties and stage workshop facilities. There was much female participation in the drama company, mostly wives and daughters of civilian staff and N.A.A.F.I. ladies who ran the large Institute and the grocery shop in the camp.

As I already had much drama experience from Queen Mary Hall, and also in a company devoted to the operas of Gilbert and Sullivan, I was very active in the various shows. Major Thompson soon noticed that I had a range of backstage talents that prompted him to say "Pickard, you're bloody useful". Praise indeed. When I finished the ammunition course, my marks for theory were very high, but my marks for practical were very low. I was not safe to let loose on ammunition. An extra place was found for me in the technical information bureau in the school where I served my remaining time. I helped with various tasks, including maintaining a huge card index system of all British ammunition from the smallest bullet to the largest bomb. It was a job that left plenty of time for work toward drama productions. I even did the bulk purchasing in London, from all the theatrical suppliers, and I got weekend rail passes to go there (and to visit a London girlfriend). I travelled from Basingstoke up to Waterloo Station. On Sunday nights my last train to Basingstoke did not connect with the Bramley train. I used to settle down in a small waiting room where a porter brought me tea and biscuits and banked the coal fire. At 5.30am on Mondays I was awakened to catch the Bramley milk train. It was all part of typical railway service in the years before the dreaded Dr. Beeching carried out the savage cuts planned by the machiavellian Ernest Marples, Minister of Transport. Marples was also a millionaire road builder. My other vivid memory of Basingstoke railway station was of a Saturday night after the 'Bramley Seedlings' had done a week of Andre Obey's *Noah* at Basingstoke Theatre. I was playing the name part, and after the last performance I ran through the streets of the town to the station, dressed as Noah. I carried my suitcase full of army uniform, and changed clothes on the train to London. Another fine production that we took to outside theatres was R.C.

Sheriff's *Journey's End*, a great play about World War One, which attracted good audiences, including retired Generals.

During 1949, 1950 and 1951 I wrote show-scripts in couplets and verse, and some serious poetry, but my second book (1951) contained no army items. *Punch Lines* was all satire, parody and mock-Chaucer. In the years since I have done poetry readings on Waterloo Station, and at most London termini. Also at the Union Jack Club and the Old Vic Theatre, both of them close to Waterloo. If I have to travel by train nowadays, I think back to the wonderful railways before Beeching, when being a railwayman was a British vocation.

I still have a friend whom I met at R.A.O.C. Bramley, fifty-eight years ago. Norman Draper was a Cambridge scholar, and North Carolina Ph.D. who has spent many decades as Professor of Statistics in Wisconsin University, Madison USA. Now 'Emeritus' he still travels to Europe for study, and he visits me each year at Weston-super-Mare. He is eleven days <u>younger</u> than me, as I remind him if he tries any scholarly jargon on me. I also exchange Christmas cards with Fred Carter, doyen of British film art directors, who was our draughtsman in the technical information bureau at Bramley. From my barrack room, two other men became university professors, and three became captains of industry. The rest became graduate professionals of all sorts. In July 1951, London, Tate & Lyle, Queen Mary Hall and the poetry world were all calling me back. It was 'Festival of Britain' time, and I started my last five years as a Londoner. Those years held the greatest single change in my whole life.

A schizophrenia in ten fragments

DECIMALISATION

For some it means innovation.
For me it's the status quo.

Don't warn me about its dangers –
It's the only way I can go.

Sometimes I find my left hand
Is unaware of my right

In their decimate and determined
Long day's journey to night.

Some say, You must need a bicycle.
Others, You must need wings

To always be five different people
Each doing two different things.

The five are not really rivals,
And even less likely mates,

But semi-deponent survivals
Of very intransitive states.

God only knows how I bear them
Under my Jester's cap.

Like rue, with a difference, I wear them
Till God sends them all for scrap.

Dedicated to all birdly, beastly and fishly poets

P(O)ETS CORNER

Read it most tenderly,
Harm not a hair;
Fashioned so slenderly.
Almost not there.

Snakes, mountain lions,
Hawks, pike and pets,
Crows, cats and piggies
Of frustrated vets.

Reynard the fox
Has at last gone to ground.
Do not give hawks the bird.
Hawk them around.

We are the learners,
The animals teach.
Not The Leech Gatherer
Now, but the leech.

Delving poetically
Into the hen
One gives up Pope
Of the study of men.

Read of them tenderly,
Harm not a hair;
Fashioned so slenderly.
Almost not there …

10

Five Fabulous Years

In mid-1951, London and all Britain were enjoying the Festival of Britain. In 1851 there was a World Exhibition in the Crystal Palace in Hyde Park. 100 years later there was an exhibition called 'Britain Can Make It' with a wide range of modern British manufacturers. But the main festival site was a fun fair at Battersea Park, land marked by the 'Skylon', a large gleaming pillar up in to the sky. All the fun of the fair was a promise fulfilled. But the timing of the work had been very tight. The Government minister responsible was Herbert Morrison, grandfather of Peter Mandelson. When sent a telegram from the Clerk of Works: NEED MORE SHOVELS STOP SOON AS POSSIBLE STOP, Morrison replied: NO MORE SHOVELS STOP TELL THE MEN TO LEAN ON EACH OTHER STOP. Best of British humour. Britain can make it.

After my release from the army, I took a month's holiday and returned to Tate & Lyle head office in August 1951. But not to Chelsea. Tate & Lyle's City office had been rebuilt at the corner of Mincing Lane, and it was there that I reported one Monday morning. I wore a newly tailored suit, a trilby hat, a carnation in the buttonhole, and carried an umbrella and a briefcase. I was T.S. Eliot's 'London Bridge Man' par excellence. The rebuilt offices had a great corner doorway into the saleroom, with a chessboard floor and steps up to the sales office, which was open-plan, with an exit to Mincing Lane at the far end. All the sugar-seeking world came in through the great front door, and we used to welcome them. On one occasion it was a Pakistani diplomat seeking 100,000 tons of granulated sugar for the people of his new country, partitioned from India. On another occasion it was three African chiefs, in full colour robes. They were from west Africa, where we sold huge tonnages of special sugars, pressed cubes, hard and symmetrical, in green boxes. At the west African ports the traders were often market mammies, super saleswomen, important to local society. From the seaports in the south to the remote regions in the North, Tate & Lyle's pressed cubes were currency in lands where paper money had never been totally trusted. Years later I was offered an agency in Accra, capital of Gold Coast (now Ghana), but, apart from the appalling climate (the White Man's Grave) it was during the dictatorship of President Nkrumah. As discretion is the better part of valour, I declined the invitation. A friend of mine was district officer at Kano, North Nigeria, a cultured man who told me much about the history, tribes and conflicts of that country. Export sales could be full of interest and excitement, as we had to know all about shipping details and insurance, whether a cargo was 'free on board', 'free alongside', or 'carriage insurance and freight'. Strange words such as dunnage and demurrage came into consideration, and occasional reference to a book of maritime law.

A point of particular interest to salesroom staff was that our office was the short cut to all the luncheon clubs of Mincing Lane, used by our managers and directors, whom we saw daily. The back door needed to be firmly closed, as spring, autumn and winter winds whistled down Mincing Lane outside that door. I posted an elegant notice on that glass door "Men and women are requested to close this door behind them. Ladies and gentlemen, of course, will". When Lord Lyle of Westbourne first read that notice I expected execution. He had a laugh at it, and carefully closed the door. Most of my sales colleagues had been twenty years with Tate & Lyle, and had at least another twenty to go. I was only twenty years of age, and did not know that I would retire at twenty-five, on the same day as two men aged sixty-five.

As at Chelsea, no senior staff came in on Saturday mornings, and junior staff in export sales held the contract book on Saturdays. It was a plain octavo book, hand-written in the scratchy style of Arthur Selby Latham, our manager. One Saturday morning I made Tate & Lyle an extra £20,000 by mistake. I was telephoned from Scandinavia by an importer seeking to confirm a contract of 20,000 tons of sugar. When I read Mr. Latham's writing to him over the 'phone I made a one shilling per hundred-weight mistake. The buyer confirmed by cable at the price I had stated. On the Monday morning I had to explain to Mr. Latham how I had misread his writing. As I had benefited the firm by £20,000, I was merely told to be careful. It could so easily have been a £20,000 loss! The sum was forty times my annual salary, and, when I 'retired' forty years early I remembered that fact. I got a generous salary rise every year after that, and there were also annual bonuses, based on the same percentage the shareholders received. Every November we got two cheques instead of one, and on one occasion my bonus was a fifth of my annual salary.

Once a month I had to visit every office, as I ran a donation scheme to 'Save The Children' Fund. Each book had 52 name spaces, and I had two books full of subscribers to the charity. The typing and secretarial office was very attractive, for obvious reasons. One of my best friendships started there, quite by chance (or by Poet Luck?). I was collecting the 'Save The Children' subscriptions when I overheard a conversation about the firm's annual dinner and dance at the Savoy Hotel in the Strand. It was always a lavish event, with fine food, marvellous music and a top class cabaret. My dread was always the dancing. I can only dance the two-left-feet Shuffle. My only rhythms are poetic metres beating in my brain. I was suddenly aware I was being paired off with a tall, shy new girl, with one foot in bulky plaster. What a perfect providence! Her name was Rosemary, the only child of two charming people who lived at Forest Hill, South London. Her father was one of the top managers of a cinema chain, and her mother also had a career in show business. They paid for us to have a taxi to the Savoy, and another taxi home again. Rosemary was a picture of loveliness in a specially made evening dress, which hid the bulky plaster. We sat out every dance, and had great conversation, as she was witty and wise. Some only children can be so much more mature than others, and she was very special. From then on, Rosemary and I were close friends, and when her father got the plum managerial job of The Regent at Brighton I used to visit them and stay for weekends. The Regent was a cinema, ballroom and restaurant all in one building, and the top floor was a large flat where Rosemary and her parents lived. It had a flat roof, high above Brighton, where we used to sunbathe for many hours, and, when her parents were out, tan our white bits also. After 1956, I only saw her in college vacations, and, soon after, I got a sad message that she had died in an accident. They say "Rosemary for remembrance", and I will never forget her.

From July 1951 I resumed my regular drama activities at Queen Mary Hall. I often went there straight from work in the City, to enjoy company and conversation with the members of the group, who were from all parts of Britain and Europe and beyond. Quite apart from drama it was our social centre and swimming club. It also had a restaurant with good cheap food. Among the foreign girls there were three sisters called Theokritoff, from St. Petersburg, Elena, Sonia and Xenia. Elena was a talented actress, and we became close friends, especially as she lived in my part of south London. The other two were equally sparky, and I attended a Russian Orthodox family wedding at a chapel in London's West End. It was a beautiful and moving ceremony. There were also three English sisters, surnamed England. Betty was blonde, a good actress and a keen cyclist, who lived near Croydon. We used to go for country rides, and, occasionally, weekends at the Camping Club by Chertsey Bridge.

The two leaders of YWCA Drama were Christine Abbott and Anne Eminton (the music director). Christine was a lively producer/director and Anne was essential, as many of our productions were musical plays. Every autumn we prepared a pantomime with an original script and music by Joan Kemp-Potter, wife of William Blezard, accompanist to Joyce Grenfell and Honor Blackman. Bill Blezard used to orchestrate music for many shows, and I was with him when he orchestrated a score for "a friend of mine, Sandy Wilson". It was *The Boyfriend*, and I heard all those songs before the public heard them. We also did the first musical of Sidney Carter (author of the *Lord of The Dance*) and Donald Swann. It was called *Lucy and The Hunter*, and was a Byronic romantic period piece, in which I had a singing part. The records of three of the songs were on sale in record shops. In 1953, for the Queen's Coronation we produced *Two Bouquets* by Herbert and Eleanor Farjeon, a delightful musical romp in the style of *The Arcadians*. A few hundred yards away Vida Hope also produced *Two Bouquets* (at the St Martins Theatre?) with professional singers. Our singing star was Barbara Firth, a talented actress who has made a world famous career in children's book illustration, notably the *Little Bear* series of books. About twenty of the drama group 'reserved' a large patch of pavement in The Mall for the Coronation. We guarded it, in relays, for two days, and we had thousands of companions, from all over the world, doing likewise. We had a fabulous picnic on the day, with much wine. The rain poured and poured. The Tannoy speakers played 'Little Red Monkey' and announced the conquest of Mount Everest by Edmund Hillary and Sherpa Tenzing. The Queen's guests, in their carriages, got as soaked as we did. Somewhere behind me, up in the grandstand, my brother and his wife had their reserved Home Office seats, but they didn't have half as much fun as we did.

Soon after Donald Swann wrote the music and played the accompaniment for *Lucy and The Hunter*, he and his school friend Michael Flanders collaborated in their brilliant revues *At the Drop of a Hat* and *Drop of Another Hat*. We were the first to hear those wonderful songs. After a long run in the West End, they took the show to America (including two years on Broadway). They also took the show to Canada, Australia and many other countries, including Scandinavia. They are as popular as Gilbert and Sullivan, which is the very highest praise. From the subtlety of 'Song of Reproduction', 'Design for Living', 'The Reluctant Cannibal' and 'Greensleeves' to the brashness of 'I'm a G-nu', 'Song of the Weather', 'Madeira M'dear' and 'The Hippopotamus Song' (Mud, Mud, Glorious Mud) their songs are a delight.

Some of their songs are sweet and sad, like 'The Slow Train'. Both Michael Flanders and Donald Swann died young, but, at least, I saved Donald for a few more years. Donald was a bouncy little man with large spectacles. He bounced on the piano stool, and he bounced when he walked. One day I met him on South Kensington Station, and he was telling me about his latest musical project. He was bouncing with excitement, and I had to grab his coat lapels to stop him bouncing backward onto the electric rails. I saved him for more years.

I could use twenty pages of this book on my Queen Mary Hall memories, but I must think of all the poetry information in the last chapters, and move on. In the mid-1950s I met the President of the YWCA, Lady Hermione Cobbold, who asked me to tape-record the Centenary of the YWCA at the Royal Albert Hall. It was good that my tape recording fame had spread so far. I enlisted the aid of another tape recorder expert, and we double-recorded the Centenary, to be safe and sure. Lady Hermione and her husband Lord Cobbold (Governor of the Bank of England) were my friends for many years. They each died at a great age, and are buried side by side. Tact forbids me to tell which one reached 100 years. Through the Cobbolds I met Lord Fisher (Archbishop of Canterbury) and chided him for brow beating Princess Margaret about her love life. He was a very dry old stick. I first met Princess Margaret when she was in the drama company of the 'Wallace Collection', Billy Wallace's collection of aristocratic friends. The backstage experts of the YWCA Drama used to help them with their great charity productions, which raised thousands of pounds each year. Sadly, Billy Wallace also died young. I was also to meet Princess Margaret in another connection. In 1954, at a City of London church, I was introduced to John Betjeman. T.S. Eliot was also at that service. They both loved all things Anglican. Betjeman was friendly, Eliot was withdrawn. I only met him once more, in strange circumstances. John Betjeman and I were friends for thirty years, until his death in 1984. John's lady love, Elizabeth Cavendish, was Lady in Waiting to Princess Margaret, so I occasionally met her when I was with John, especially after John moved to the same Chelsea road as Elizabeth, in his later years.

My twenty-fourth year (1955) saw the biggest change in my life, and a move in a different direction. For many years I had enjoyed all the heavens of hedonism, wine, women and song. I had even been gang-raped twice by two different quartets of 'Sloane Rangers' who shared large flats in Kensington. In each case I was a pliant prisoner for a whole weekend. I know about Stockholm Syndrome, falling for your torturers. At a less drastic level, I had friends among BOAC stewardesses, who lived at Chelsea Cloisters, luxury service flats near my first place of work. In between flights, they loved to give cheese fondu parties, with limitless baguette bread and a huge pot of melted cheese. Any bit of bread that fell into the pot was penalised by the removal of a garment. By midnight or even eleven p.m., the parties became very interesting. I guess that some of the bits of bread were deliberately dropped. The same group of girls always had a party at the Chelsea Arts Ball, held in the Albert Hall each New Year's Eve from 8pm to 5 am. Thousands attended, all in fancy dress, chosen according to a theme. Huge tableaux, by every art school, were put together only to be broken up in the first hours of the New Year. Out with the Old, in with the New. There were always four famous bands, and in the early 1950s I heard all the top bands play, including Ivy Benson and her Girl Band. Every stage and film star was at the Chelsea Arts Ball, and when food and drink ran out, one gatecrashed a bigger, richer party where nobody noticed the intruders. At midnight, thousands of balloons descended from the roof, and the arts tableaux were destroyed. Two tableaux that I remember were a huge champagne glass (shallow shape) in which swam (topless) the beautiful young 'Lido Jenny' who had been arrested for bathing topless at the Serpentine Lido in Hyde Park. At midnight she was carried off over someone's shoulder. In another year, when I was in velvet garb (Spirit of Poetry) I ran through a Roman Temple, losing my Quill Pen but gaining a Vestal Virgin to carry off till dawn. I am exhausted even to think about it now.

The year 1955 was to bring me a new use for wine, a new attitude to women, and many new songs. It all started on the last train out of Victoria Station to Gipsy Hill, on my way home. As usual, I only caught the train by sprinting along Victoria Street from the Central Hall, where I had attended a meeting. I leapt into the train without looking, and found myself in a dingy carriage where two young men were in the opposite corner. Very soon, one of the young men was convulsing and dribbling down his chin. I had been to a Christian meeting in the Central Hall, Westminster, and then to a café to discuss the matters of the Meeting. I was full of thoughts about basic Christianity, not the usual concern of my weekday evenings. The healthy one of the two young men seemed embarrassed, not for himself, but for his friend. He explained that they had been soldiers in the recent Korean War, and that the handicapped man had saved his friend's life. After leaving the army, he felt obliged to care for his damaged friend who had saved him. His friend's self-sacrifice placed him under obligation. Two of the hymns of the Central Hall Meeting had been "What a Friend we have in Jesus" and "Were you there when they crucified my Lord?" No, I wasn't, but I suddenly understood the enormity of the sacrifice made by Jesus Christ. For me. After the two young men got out of the train, I was alone with my thoughts. I had a few minutes before my home station. I knelt on the dusty floor and prayed to understand Christ's supreme sacrifice. As I walked up the steep hill to my home, I thought about what I had done, and what I had to do. The next morning I looked at the knees of the trousers where I knelt. They had large grey patches of ingrained dirt. I left those knees grubby because they were a reminder of my intention. It took me some study of the Gospels and Acts of the Apostles. I attended confirmation classes. I was praying daily. I was in the hands of the Holy Spirit, a good guide.

THE TURNING POINT

On 23rd. April 1616
(It was a dull day)
England turned
On its axis.

While Stratford people
Passed quietly
About their business
While Shakespeare died

A plain young man
Entered Cambridge
As sober in manner
As his surroundings.

Oliver Cromwell
Learning to learn,
Learning to be
A Lord Protector.

It was as if
The Lord had repeated
I will not leave you
Comfortless.

ON THE SIDE OF THE ANGELS

It is not pride that makes me doubt the ape
As ancestor, nor prejudice that tells
Me confidently, "No cathedral bells
Summon the chimpanzee to his escape".

My stance of body, and my frame of mind
Aren't such as a Behaviourist asserts
Responsive only to rewards and hurts,
Being to all more subtle matters blind.

A kind of anger causes me to speak
Of grace and genius, of love and art
As things no physical and pumping heart
Engenders. All around me are unique

Reminders of my own uniqueness, seen
As only I can see them; just as you,
With your eyes, can authenticate as true
A picture, with no dark glass in between.

Necessity has not produced a child
At all. And all the dirt of all the world,
And every hurtful phrase that can be hurled
At me, still leaves me undefiled.

One day you'll laugh, and say of me, "He died,
Like everybody else, and was disposed
Of, flesh and bone. The episode is closed."
Not so. For I am on the angels' side.

11

The Truth Shall Set You Free

The Holy Spirit is a smooth operator. When the Spirit moves it moves into overdrive. In 1954 I was a casual Christian, or so I thought. I had done some correspondence course studies in religion since I left school. I thought I was doing those courses for cultural information, but Someone Else knew better. By 1955 I was a confirmed communicant in my parish at Christ Church, Gipsy Hill. I had also joined the Tate & Lyle Christian Union, a small group of active believers at head office and the Thames-side refineries. Through them I had helped in a Mission in the Silvertown area, led by the Rev. David Sheppard and helpers from the Mayflower Centre in that area. David Sheppard had captained England at cricket, and was later the Anglican Bishop of Liverpool, where he had close collaboration with the Roman Catholic Bishop for many years. The only three cities where I have done poetry readings in both Anglican and Roman Catholic cathedrals are Liverpool (once in each cathedral), Birmingham (twice in each cathedral) and Bristol (many times in each cathedral, during three decades). Bristol Anglican Cathedral was very sympathetic to Christian poetry events. In addition to famous Christian poems, I read several Charles Causley poems such as 'The Bread Man' and 'Timothy Winters' (for events with children). I once read 'Timothy Winters' from the pulpit of Bristol Anglican Cathedral, and most of the packed congregation joined in the last lines, "Amen, Amen, Amen, Amen – Timothy Winters, Lord, Amen". It was an exciting experience. I had permanent permission from Charles Causley to use his poems. We also did several readings together at Bristol and Swindon. Bristol's Roman Catholic Cathedral (Saints Peter and Paul) I saw built in Pembroke Road, a stone's throw from the publishers of this book. Teams of readers did themed events in that circular

Cathedral, with myself and notable presenters from the BBC and HTV.

Having taken the Christian plunge, I learned to swim strongly with the tide. All my prayers seemed to be guiding me towards ordained ministry. I took all my educational certificates to a discussion with my vicar, the Rev. Stanley Longes, at Christ Church, Gipsy Hill. He was enthusiastically helpful, and he arranged for me to attend a selection weekend at Farnham Castle, where I was selected. The vicar then got me invitations to Merton College, Oxford and to Selwyn College, Cambridge for possible theology courses. I spent enjoyable weekends at each place, but could not obtain a three-year grant. I then received an invitation from a College at Bristol, Clifton Theological College, on Stoke Hill, Stoke Bishop. They also found me a grant covering all my needs for three years. It was a small college in a lovely old house built in 1669, Charles II Restoration times. The college motto was VERITAS VOS IN LIBERTATEM VINDICABIT – The Truth Shall Set You Free (St. John's Gospel 8.32), and it certainly had. In the space of a year I had gone from being a new communicant to being an accepted ordinand.

It was arranged that I should start at Bristol in September 1956, with the aim to graduate in July 1959, for Michaelmas 1959 Ordination, in late September. But first I had to 'retire' from Tate & Lyle at 25 years of age. Retirement day was a memorable one. Two men aged 65 were leaving on the same day, and the boardroom tables had three large piles of gifts appropriate to each of us. Theirs were books and hobbies items. Mine (as I would get no pension) were different, many useful books and some envelopes containing cheques totalling hundreds of pounds. The books included a fifteen-volume set of *The Treasury of David* C.H. Spurgeon's Commentary on all 150 of the Psalms, given me by the directors. The cheques, from many offices, came from almost everyone at Head Office, and secured my financial needs for several years ahead. I gave a short speech, as did the two other men, who had spent fifty years with Tate & Lyle, since Edwardian times early in the century.

My good fortune was boundless. When I went to a second-hand shop in West Norwood to buy a trunk for my long stay in Bristol, I found a very large brassbound cabin trunk with all its keys. It had shipping labels from all over the world pasted to it, and only cost me £5. When it was delivered to my home I found that one side was a wardrobe with sliding hangers. The other side had seven large drawers, and the bottom was full of large operatic scores, words and music. The soprano parts were pencilled. Some operatic diva had travelled all over the world with that trunk. I found a music shop and sold all the scores for three times what I had paid for the trunk. Even opera smiled on me. My father laughed heartily.

The trunk was packed and sent to Bristol. On a beautiful day in late September 1956 I went from Paddington to Bristol Temple Meads to start my long love affair with Bristol. Fifty years on, the flame still burns. At college I was given a ground-floor room at terrace level, and the splendid window was the original 17th-century one. It looked out onto the lower garden and the fine greenhouse swimming pool, always very warm in summer. My room had a large walk-in wardrobe where I kept the trunk and many other things. The room was superbly centrally placed. It was only ten yards from the comfortable common room, fifteen yards from a bathroom, and near the stone stairs to the front hall. But I could have had a problem, had I been a light sleeper. I discovered that my room, with its ancient window, was the main after-hours access used by everybody to come in after the front door was locked at 10.p.m. Fortunately I was a very heavy sleeper, like a log. Week by week, for three years, thirty or forty men traversed my room in the late and early hours, but I slept soundly through it all.

My room was directly below the study of the principal, the Rev. Llewellyn Roberts, a saintly man with a marked lisp in his voice. His wife was a splendidly motherly soul to us all. On one occasion he was explaining the structure of an evangelistic mission that twenty of us were going on. Regardless (or unaware) of lisp, he explained that we would have several SECTIONAL meetings, which sounded much more naughty than that. How the twenty of us refrained from collapsing in helpless mirth I do not know. Llewellyn Roberts deserved a much more saintly collection of students than we were. His vice-principal was the Rev. Alex Motyer, an auburn Irishman of great Hebrew scholarship, much wit and high humour. It was as if Dublin had sent us another Jonathan Swift. He also had a charming wife and two intelligent sons. I can still remember his Christmas sermon at Bristol Cathedral on "What is the X in Xmas?" I last heard him ministering at Hove, near Brighton, and I note from Crockford's clerical directory that his son Stephen (whom I taught archery when he was seven years old) has had an academic theological career as distinguished as his father. Archery was part of my responsibility as sports secretary of the college. The main sports were cricket, rugby and soccer, where we played many matches. I played in goal for the soccer team, and we were in two college cup finals in my three years, losing one and winning one. I still have my cup medal. I was also responsible for cleaning and chlorinating the swimming pool, of which I made great use. There was also croquet on the large front lawn, but I left that to the men who understood it. I find it difficult to relate "the meek shall inherit the earth" with bashing your opponent's ball thirty yards into some bushes. I also played badminton at church halls and university courts. I like to think that I invented the twenty-feet high badminton 'rocket' serve, just as I wore 'Mickey Mouse' gloves for goalkeeping long before any professional footballer did. I also had my bicycle at College, and rode everywhere, including to my parents' home in south London, a ride of 120 miles that I did in seven hours, with a meal break. I made that ride many times by day and night, and wrote a long poem about it for John Betjeman.

A shorter and more frequent ride was to the National Nautical School at Portishead (now made into an exclusive residential complex) where I was assistant to the chaplain. Each time I cycled to Portishead I had to use Pill Ferry across the river Avon, a small boat with a muddy plank. To walk that plank with bike on shoulder was a perilous procedure, as the tide was fast. The only alternative was the much longer route via Brunel's Clifton Suspension Bridge. The town of Portishead was powerfully Protestant. One of my fellow students, Roger Sainsbury (now a bishop) married Jenny Carey from a family of Portishead Protestants. Another local Christian was a farmer who ran a gospel hall where I was active, near Bristol Docks. In autumn 1956 thousands of Hungarians fled from Russian tanks in Budapest, and four hundred of them ended up in Bristol, poor and jobless and wordless. I volunteered to teach 20 of them at the farmer's gospel hall. How would I do it? We had no word of each other's language. I sent to the Bible Society for 21 Hungarian New Testaments and 21 English New Testaments. I also bought an English/Hungarian dictionary at the University bookshop. We then learned the whole of the New Testament (except Revelation). Their English became good. Yea, verily and behold, it did! And it came to pass in those days that they all got jobs, and most of them became Christians. Some of them soon had their own businesses. I did all that in addition to my intensive studies, including learning New Testament Greek.

Across Bristol Downs from my college were two other theological colleges, Tyndale Hall (male and muscular no-nonsense Christianity) run by the Bible Churchman's Missionary Society, and there was Dalton House Women's College. Those two colleges are now amalgamated with my old college to form Trinity College in the big house where I lived and studied, 1956 to 1959. Trinity College has additional buildings, and is much bigger and much more international than my college ever was. It has had Bishops and an Archbishop of Canterbury, George Carey, now retired and living in Clifton, Bristol. I can admire all the achievements of Trinity College, but it would never suit me. I need a small selective set-up in all things.

By summer 1959 I had passed all my theological exams, and graduated on a splendidly sunny day in July. My new academic hood and new robes were all ready to be worn. I was looking and praying for a possible parish in my home diocese of Southwark for the next three years. But there were Bristol matters to be resolved, particularly in personal relationship. And there were urgent matters when a starting parish was found in South London, and all the legalities toward ordination as deacon at Southwark Cathedral by London Bridge. In both the personal and parochial senses, the man who had been 'vacant' had become 'engaged'.

THE OTHER HALF

Alight with caution.
Which I did.
And looking upward
At the bus which hid
The moon
I saw
Another world
Of faces,
Each one on a neck
All on the upper deck
I never saw before.

Up there, My God,
Are folk
Who smoke
And joke
And do not care,
Who would not
Think obscene
The question
How far
Can one go
On a number eighteen?

One day,
I vowed myself,
I'll take
The courage
Of an indrawn breath
And climb
That stair,
Perhaps up there
Is life and downstairs
Death?

CANDIDA

She did not know
The secret
In the poet's heart.

He did not know
The secret,
But he played the part.

We did not know
the poet was aware
of simultaneous
Heaven and despair.

BRIXTON

The snow lay deep
On roads and roofs and gardens.

Unsullied by footstep
Early in the day.

The writing on the wall said
KEEP BRITAIN WHITE

I raised my head
And breathed
The wintry air.

There was
No hint
Of a thaw.

12

Some Enchanted Evening

In many hundreds of parishes one of the church powerhouses is 'The Over Twenty Club'. So it was at St. Mary Magdalene, Stoke Bishop, Bristol in the 1950s, and so it was at St. Matthias, Upper Tulse Hill, London in the 1960s. From 1956 to 1959, only a few hundred yards from my college, I went to Sunday evening meetings of the Over Twenties. The age boundaries were usually flexible. Mature 18s and 19s were acceptable, and the upper age limit was elastic. If you were an asset beyond 30 years of age, you were welcome to hang on in there. In 1958 I was 27 years of age, and the chair (person) of Stoke Bishop Over Twenties was a young woman school teacher, Jean Goodwin, a year younger than myself. Her father, Bill Goodwin, was a benefactor of the church, and her lovely little mother, Irene, was very welcoming to the parish Over Twenties. They often went, en masse, to breakfast at the Goodwins' house after early morning communion service.

One Sunday evening it was my turn to give a talk to the Over Twenty Club, and I must have made a reasonable job of it because I was thanked both officially and personally by Jean Goodwin. She was a foot shorter than me, but full of life and laughter. She taught infants at Uphill Primary School, Weston-super-Mare, the school where our elder grand daughter now attends. In winter Jean lived with a family at Weston, but in spring and summer she drove her car from Bristol to Weston every day. My interest in Jean became stronger with the passing weeks, and I used my room window in the EXIT direction after 10pm some evenings. I was always in college for 'lock-up', but often out immediately after 10pm. Her parents were kind and amused by our growing friendship, and her younger brother, Peter, was a pain, but younger brothers usually mock sister's boyfriends. By Christmas 1958, my last Christmas at college, we became engaged to be married. In autumn 1958 I got my friend and Norwood neighbour, Leslie Randles, to make a gold and ruby engagement ring. Our day of engagement was 28th December – Holy Innocents Day! Jean's father had arranged for a family weekend outing to London to see the new musical *My Fair Lady* at Drury Lane Theatre. We saw the original English stars, Julie Andrews, Rex Harrison, Stanley Holloway, Zena Dare, Leonard Weir and Robert Coote, and we watched them from a box near the stage. It was a grand, glorious (and expensive) day out.

Since my Christian conversion I was a reformed character, mainly toward women. I became a traditional swain, wooing and pursuing Jean with all the diligence of a devotee. It has been my behaviour to her for the past forty-nine years. Even at age twenty-seven, love's young dream is fine, but many practical matters needed to be decided. My future Bishop of Southwark, Mervyn Stockwood, did not allow beginners in Anglican ministry to be beginners in marriage, so the wedding date would be a year later than my first ordination, September 1959. The chancellor of the Southwark diocese helped me to an important decision. What's in a name? Shakespeare's question has several answers. The chancellor pointed out that if I had two surnames (which I did) I would spend my entire ministry being called 'Mr Priestley-Pickard', many times a day, 365 days each year. The prospect was so awful that I had my surname officially registered as 'Pickard' and the Priestley became a prename after 1959. It was a sobering thought that few of those Sloane Rangers, debutantes, and wealthy women who delighted me till age twenty-four would have supplicated a single surname, especially as most of them had two surnames, and some had three. In the 1950s , such things still had some significance. My very down-to-earth mother had always clung to her three surnames, Horsley Priestley Pickard, especially as the richest man who sought her teenage hand in marriage was called Ramsbottom. One of my lovers, ten years older than me, had proposed marriage to me, and offered me a Chelsea house (bought in my own name) as token of her devotion. I was touched, but not moved. I knew all about her dollars-with-strings, and twenty-two was no age to be tied up with strings. Nowadays that Chelsea house would cost much more than a million pounds. Possibly two million.

So, the newly named, newly graduated, newly robed William prepared to become a deacon. Mervyn Stockwood always called me William, never Bill. He had no warm way of saying "William". As did Gladstone with Queen Victoria, he addressed me like a public meeting. The last time I ever saw Mervyn Stockwood, he was with Malcolm Muggeridge and the Monty Python team on television discussing the film *The Life of Brian* in 1979. He was pontificating then, and I have no doubt that he pontificated to the last, in his elegant retirement at Bath. Mervyn Stockwood's chaplain, Michael Mayne was kinder to me, and I often met him at the Bishop's House near Streatham. Thirty-five years later (on 11th November 1996) I was invited to Westminster Abbey by Michael Mayne, by now Dean of the Abbey, to attend the dedication by Lady Mary Wilson, of John Betjeman's memorial in Poets' Corner. Michael was a fine author, and had many years as B.B.C. head of Religious Broadcasting. I always thought of Michael and Mervyn as 'Good Cop, Bad Cop'. At a clergy day in Southwark Cathedral every priest could comment on the diocese (and Bishop). You stood up, announced your parish, and said your say. An elderly priest (safely headed for retirement) spent several minutes mauling Mervyn. Then a quiet little priest got up to speak. When he announced his parish as 'The Good Shepherd' the hundreds of clergy collapsed in hearty laughter. The contrast with Mervyn.

But Mervyn was a showman. He had more razzmatazz than Barnum and Bailey. His Dean organised a good Michaelmas 1959 ordination. I only knew two of my fellow deacons that year. Richard Salmon had been a fellow student at Clifton Theological College, and was generous with his time and help. He drove an Austin Seven car called 'DORCAS', because, as in Acts of Apostles, she was "full of good works". He went to his first curacy at St. Michael, Blackheath Park, then to St. Albans diocese, then to

Malaysia to minister for a decade. His last parish was Congresbury, Puxton and Hewish in North Somerset, and he and his wife Helen live in retirement at Hutton, only a mile from where I am writing this. He is four years younger than me and still quite active. The other 1959 deacon I knew was John Conway Meek, two years younger than me, whose first curacy was at Immanuel with St. Anselm, Streatham, near Streatham Common. He spent much of his ministry at Canterbury and York, where he was canon and prebendary of York Minster. He died in 2002, a friend I was sad to lose.

I was ordained to serve at St. Matthias, Upper Tulse Hill, near Brixton, an area that I knew well. I was only a few miles from my parents' Norwood home, and spent my weekly day off with them. My vicar was Rev. James Headland, eleven years older than me, a former tool-maker and Royal Navy man, who studied at my Bristol college. We both laboured under the problem that the previous vicar had been massively charismatic, and deeply loved by one and all. He had also related closely with the secular sur-roundings. Jim Headland was a tough-love vicar, and I was in the difficult position of piggy-in-the-middle, and had to maintain discreet diffidence. It was no fun for a first timer, especially as I lived in the attic floor of the vicarage, and all callers to me had to pass through the residential part of the vicarage. To hear the previous vicar praised by comparison is standard experience, but to have to tread a tightrope of loyalty for three years is no fun. What was pleasant was the strength of the youth work raised by the previous incumbent, and kept going by our splendid Sister Matthias, a uniformed lay-worker of great ability and charm. Both young and old (and in between) loved and respected her. I never saw her take any time for herself, so I have the impression she was always on duty. My predecessor as curate was a very posh young man, Stephen Trapnell, from a famous Bristol family. Stephen had degrees of Cambridge and Virginia Theological Seminary, U.S.A. He later worked in connection with evangelism and Rwanda. The only thing that I remember was that he drove a

Messerschmitt Beetle car. The curate before Stephen Trapnell was Peter Schneider, who had notable ministry to Jews in the Holy land. I never met him, but one oft-repeated tale concerns early communion at 8am, on Sundays. Like myself, Peter Schneider was a heavy sleeper, and he frequently appeared at the early communion with two inches of striped pyjama trousers below his dark clerical trousers. Why did he not go to bed in his day trousers on Saturday nights? Both Peter and Stephen were very good at certain aspects of Christian ministry, and no good at others, exactly as I am. It is one of the great problems of parishes that there are inevitable gaps in ministry (except in Victorian times, when some parishes had six Curates and most parishes had two, chosen to complement).

My first year at St. Matthias sometimes made me think of how the Saint got chosen. After the departure of Judas, the close disciples cast lots for his replacement. "AND THE LOT FELL UPON MATTHIAS". How many times did I feel the truth of that! All new curates are assumed to be mugs. Certainly by vagrants and hoboes. The news spread like wild fire among the 'travellers' of the Brighton Road, only a few hundred yards away. "St Matthias Parish has got a NEW CURATE". A steady stream of vagrants turned up on the vicarage doorstep, but they only rang MY bell. They then told me an amazing variety of reasons why they need £1, £3, £5, £10 or more, for some purpose that could not be postponed. I kept my back pocket stocked with shilling coins, enough for tea and a sandwich or for a bus ride across London. I would give each tale-teller a shilling and point him to Brixton Hill where a friendly café sold sandwiches, and buses to Tavistock Square stopped. At Tavistock Square was a social security office open 24 hours a day, 365 days a year. They could tell their tale to the social security officers. I wonder whether any ever did? But I hoped they enjoyed their tea and sandwich. At Christmas 1959, my only solitary Christmas, I enjoyed at the Brixton Hill Café, a huge Christmas lunch of soup, turkey and three vegetables, Christmas pudding and custard, and a cup of coffee, all for 4/6d (22 pence).

Although it was well known in the parish that I was engaged to be married, it did not prevent a wide range of women from bombarding my bachelor state with all the wiles of wifery – cooking, sewing, chocolate, even clothing. The clergyman in Gilbert and Sullivan's *The Sorcerer* sings of how "Time was when love and I were well acquainted … I was a pale young curate then". It was as true in 1960 as it was in 1880, except that I was nearly 30, not pale, and engaged to be married. I wish I could say that none of my supplicants were associated with the church, but most of them were. From the boldest teenagers to maiden ladies approaching fifty years, I got cakes, puddings, pies, biscuits, chocolates, books (including some saucy ones), kitchen items, shirts, cushions, and even some vests! One lady gave me a set of curtains (obviously measured before I arrived), and one blushing nurse was brought by her monstrous mother who owned a local nursing home. They needed a 'chaplain', and I could have a room on the premises! The younger woman was embarrassed, but her mother took much dissuading from her plan. One very beautiful woman about my age, who lived just outside our Parish, kept seeking counselling. I contacted her own vicar, who was baffled by her. She moved to Chelsea, and later committed suicide. Why does funny farce tip over into tragedy? Because farce IS tragedy, happening to other people.

Two middle-aged friends, married but childless, lived a few yards from the vicarage, in a bungalow by the gates of Tulse Hill School. The school was known as 'Gaitskell's Dream' when he was Labour Party Leader (it was a HUGE comprehensive school). Everyone except Gaitskell came to regard it as a nightmare rather than a dream. My friends' bungalow was broken into by pupils of the school countless times, and defaced in many ways, but Ted and Marjorie were very resolute. She was head of a girls' school. They had a 400-year-old country cottage in Sussex, at Mountfield, near Battle. Three weeks in October 1960 (free of charge) was their wedding present to Jean and me. The Elizabethan cottage was a perfect place for a honeymoon couple. Most Monday mornings our bell at the vicarage would ring, and we would find some gift from Sussex, brought back by Ted and Marjorie. He was a travelling salesman for a clothing company. They also gave us our 1961 and 1962 holidays at their lovely cottage, free of charge. My parents went there, and our first-born Jane went with us in 1962, age six months. Such kindness from people we hardly knew. Twenty years later, when we lived at Bristol, Doctor Ian Bailey and his wife Winifred gave us many two-week holidays at their cottage at the gates of Wordsworth's Rydal Mount, Grasmere, Cumbria. They were near neighbours, who sadly died young. Their daughter Claire is now a consultant at Bristol Eye Hospital.

FAMILY ALLOWANCES

Spare a thought,
For the pram-pushing
Needy.

Fathers need
Their little
Status symbols.

Mothers need
Their little
Accessories.

Grandparents need
Their assurances
Of immortality.

Aunts and Uncles
Need their
Outlets for charity.

Only schoolteachers
Need children
Other than as

Status symbols, accessories,
Assurances or outlets,
And for what do they need them?

STOKE HOUSE 1669

on Stoke Hill, Stoke Bishop
(now Trinity College)

Restoration was in the air,
Plague and fire forgotten
And the Commonwealth
Which the common folk
Scarcely saw as theirs
Was done with
And over.

The builders' materials,
Straight beams
And twisted portals
And all that protects
Preserves and cossets
More fortunate mortals
Lay in clover.

Destiny shaped its ends;
Indeed, not so much
Destiny as Divinity.
From slavestop to
Salvation Station
Dedicated to the Holy
(And Undivided) Trinity.

13

Waiting At The Church

For a year I had been waiting at the church. Waiting to become a priest. Waiting to become a married man. Waiting for my lovely Jean. September 1960 gave Mervyn Stockwood, the Bishop of Southwark, full rein for his striking showmanship. He would hold the first-ever televised ordination, in his cathedral. And in the front pews would be the recently married Princess Margaret and the Earl of Snowdon. It was a glorious prospect, except for the ordinands. On top of ordinary clothes, a clergyman wears a thick cassock and a white surplice and a very long scarf and an academic hood. Add many thousands of candlepower of T.V. lighting and you have a form of torture not far removed from Hell. It ain't 'arf 'ot, Mum. And it went on for hours. All seen by the amazed British public. We could have worn placards, 'As seen on television'.

Every time I am caught in car headlights, I think I am being ordained for a third time. Even to think about it makes me sweat. As I said to the radical Bishop of Woolwich, John Robinson (who specialised in 'retreats'), "If you are so avant garde, why are you always in retreat?" He could not give me an answer. Perhaps he put it in one of his best selling books. Back at the parish I was allowed to celebrate holy communion. And I was only two weeks away from another communion, holy matrimony. On Saturday 8th October 1960, Jean and I were married at St. Mary Magdalene, Stoke Bishop, Bristol. It poured with rain all day, but we hardly noticed. We were on top of the cloud, not underneath it. We were married free of charge, because we were the first service conducted by the new Vicar, Leslie Williams, but he had the benefit of all our flowers for his induction the previous evening. Fair shares for all. But we got more than our fair share of sermon. A very earnest tutor at my college, John McKechnie, preached for about twenty five minutes. Add on the twenty minutes the bride was late (because the car broke down) and the time it took to awaken the congregation, the reception started an hour late. It was held in a huge marquee on the front lawn of her parents' house. Fortunately there were canvas corridors to the house, because the rain went on all day. That night we were booked in at The Mitre at Shaftesbury, and Jean drove brilliantly to get us there in time for dinner. After dinner we went to the cinema. The film was *The Nun's Story*, a missionary hospital in the Belgian Congo, with Audrey Hepburn and Peter Finch smouldering at each other all over the screen. We almost ran back to the hotel. We wanted to do some smouldering, but the bed had creaky springs and we finished in a heap of hysterical laughter. We had three weeks in an Elizabethan cottage to make up for lost time. For at least an hour each day we went out to get some fresh air. Very healthy place, Mountfield. As Pa Larkins would have said, it was "perfick".

Jean's presence made our attic flat a new world, and she was soon more of an asset to the parish than I was. Sister Mathias was twice Jean's age, but they used to giggle like two schoolgirls. I never asked them why. Jean got a teaching job at St. George The Martyr School, Elephant and Castle, and travelled by bus from Brixton Hill. On the first school morning she had to retreat into a shop doorway as a woman with a carving knife chased a man through the streets. The school class was also a shock. The children told her they had got rid of eight teachers in a month. Jean resolved not to be ousted, and she wasn't. When she left the school, a year later, to have our first child, those little street urchins cried for her to stay. She is a genius with children. One of those children had a criminal record that included burglary at Waterloo Station! The large, lumbering caretaker, who lived alone in the school basement, used to buy her a pint of milk every day throughout her pregnancy, "For the babby", he said, embarrassed. The school headmaster was also very clever with tough children, and he ran an educational business from the school, as a sideline. One of the teachers, Petronella, was 6 feet 3 inches tall and the niece of the Bishop of Coventry. She produced Shakespeare's *A Midsummer Night's Dream* with her class. Magical. When Petronella was about to fly to India to teach, a 6 foot 5 inch suitor stopped her, and married her at Coventry Cathedral. He was Robin McNaghten, master of Wall House at Eton College, and later headmaster of Sherborne, in Dorset. We visited them once at Wall House for a day, and were not impressed by what we saw of Eton College.

Jean went into East Dulwich Hospital to have our firstborn, Rosemary Jane, who arrived on 1st March 1962. Two days later I was smashed off my bike by a taxi driven by a man asleep at the wheel. Where was I taken? East Dulwich Hospital. The following morning I was taken in a wheelchair to see Jean and Jane. Jean was duly amazed at the lengths I would go to, just to see her. Back at the parish, members of the youth club used to ask to wheel Jane in her big high perambulator. One of the wheelers was Mick Buck, an electrician 'biker', all in black leathers. He loved wheeling Jane about. I think it greatly impressed the girl members. When the youth club massively renovated the church hall, Mike Buck replaced all the electrics at his own expense. Most of the youth club were that wonderful, and Jean and I took them to many places for weekends and a week's holiday at Weston-super-Mare. We also made several weekend visits to an ancient stately home, Ashburnham, on the site of the Battle of Hastings (1066 and all that). It was the seat of the Earls of Ashburnham (line defunct), though there was also a baronetcy created in 1661, and the 12th Baronet, Sir Denny Ashburnham lived not very far away at Broomham, Hastings, Sussex. Ashburnham was the home of the Rev. John Bickersteth and his Swiss wife Marlies, while they supervised its transformation into a Christian Conference Centre. Jean and I and the youth club used to do very basic tasks toward the new centre, and in the evenings consider Christian matters. The great house had its own church, a short walk away. One Sunday morning Jean helped Marlies with the washing up after early communion. Jean was amazed at the weight of the plate. It was solid gold. The house had a Van Dyck portrait of the 1st Earl of Ashburnham, an orangery made by Inigo Jones, and grounds landscaped by Capability Brown. Although St. Matthias parish had some fine Christian adults, especially in the 'Over Twenties', it was the youth club, and their active faith, that I have particularly remembered of the years 1959 to 1962 at Upper Tulse Hill. One incident I also vividly remember. Halfway between the vicarage and the church was the new school of Holy Trinity, our adjacent parish. Holy Trinity, Tulse Hill, was for some years the Parish of the Rev. Dr. John Sentamu, now Archbishop of York. Earlier, in 1961, the head teacher asked me to do weekly lessons, every Friday afternoon, on Biblical themes. I decided to tell the exciting stories of the Acts of the Apostles. One Friday afternoon the sky was dark and thundery. I was telling the oldest children how an angry Pharisee, Saul, set off for Damascus to persecute Christians. On the road to Damascus he was struck to the ground by heavenly action, and was taken to Damascus where he became the Paul who wrote many great letters to the churches at Rome, Corinth and other places. Just as I described Saul being struck down, a flash of lightning hit the classroom and great claps of thunder shook the school, as a thunderbolt broke the roof of a nearby house. Ever after that people looked at me differently. Some crossed the road toward me, others away from me. Thunder and lightning are small reminders of God's power.

On the day that Jean and I and baby Jane were packing to leave Upper Tulse Hill, we had a visit from Richard Salmon, on his day off from his parish at Blackheath. He bought us fish and chips, and took carloads of our goods to my parents' home at Norwood. His last load was the three Pickards, and he had tea with us and my parents, before his drive back to Blackheath. A good friend.

My second curacy was all arranged at the parish of St. Helen's, Rainham, Essex, which had two daughter churches, Wennington and one on a large housing estate. I was to live at Wennington and be responsible for its church, but nothing worked out as planned. The house we were promised was not ready. It was still not ready six months later, when we left in 1963. The winter of 1962/3 was one of the worst in recent years, with months of snow and ice. I was by then a car driver and our Morris Traveller was a lifeline to get about in appalling conditions. We were loaned a Georgian ruin of a house, in the middle of a field, but the rector of Rainham never did anything to fulfil the arrangements. We struggled for six months with an asthmatic baby in a freezing ruin, but had to leave because the rector of Rainham could never be contacted. He was a popular speaker, with many contacts, home and abroad, and was often away. The other curate also left at the same time as us, and went to an Edinburgh parish. I have no liking for Essex. When I eventually got the pay for my time in Essex, we were able to move back to Bristol and live with Jean's parents. I soon received an invitation from an evangelistic organisation called The Shaftesbury Crusade, named after the great reformer, the 7th Earl of Shaftesbury, whose memorial is the statue at Piccadilly Circus in London. Because English only has one word for 'love', the statue had to be Eros! The Greeks had four words for different loves. The Shaftesbury Crusade had old premises in a part of Bristol known as The Dings, and had long Boys Brigade and rugby football associations. They had another crusade church and hall on the Lockleaze Housing Estate, Bristol, near Gloucester Road. The Crusade hall had eleven acres of sports fields where the rugby was played. The Rev. Norman Voice was warden of the original Crusade in The Dings, and I was to look after the new centre and work at Lockleaze. I moved my family to a bungalow at nearby Patchway (where I would later teach at the High School) and started my new task. There were Sunday services, Boys Brigade parades, many clubs for men, women and children, Sunday schools and estate work. My full time assistant was an elderly lady who had spent many years in China, mostly at Shanghai, where she had taught a little girl called Peggy Hookham, who became the great prima ballerina Dame Margot Fonteyn. Mrs Boaler lived on the Lockleaze estate, which had been built by a British company that her husband had worked for in China. The estate also had Anglican and Presbyterian Churches, so there was plenty of Christian witness in the area. The Church of St. James produced the Christian 'musical' *A Man Dies*, which was a great success, with performances at London's Royal Albert Hall, and big sales of long-playing records. My great event of 1964 was the birth, in January, of our second daughter, Heather Ann. She was born at Southmead Hospital on 29th January, and joined the three of us in the bungalow at Patchway.

Busy though I was at Shaftesbury Lockleaze, I was already thinking of more radical forms of ministry, and regretted that England had no tradition of worker priests, such as many Continental countries have. One of the French Movements produced a book *La Rue est Mon Eglise* (The Street is My Church), which is about as radical as one can get. Rather less radical is to work in personnel and welfare in a factory, and in my second year at Lockleaze I received an invitation to take up such a post in a factory in Avonmouth Docks. At the same time the Shaftesbury Crusade had a financial problem, and wanted to rationalise all its activities with much more lay leadership. It suited them and me to part, so we parted. To get to Avonmouth, I needed to live that side of Bristol, so we moved to a quiet road off Parry's Lane, to 21 Rylestone Grove, where we lived 26 years, until we left Bristol. It was a superb detached house, built by Stride, the top quality house builders, in 1935. We were only the second owners. We were very lucky to get the house for £7,000. When we sold it, in 1990, we got £140,000 for it, due to a quarter of a century of price inflation. The really big houses in Rylestone Grove are the even numbers across the road, only six of them (2–12) and only fourteen odd numbers, 20 houses in all, a separate little world. The infant and junior schools nearby were among the best in Bristol. Our daughters had a great start in life. Jean's parents lived only 200 yards away, and my parents often stayed with them, so we had a full family quarter-century.

My six years of personnel and welfare work at Avonmouth (1964–1969 inclusive) only ended when the factory was taken over and closed. I had had thousands of interviews with workers about their personal problems, and I was always able to find a Christian agency to help them. I was in the English tradition of worker priest, less radical! Precisely as the factory closed, the Post Office was being severed from Government control and was offering three year in-service personnel courses leading to the Institute of Personnel Management. There was a new Regional Headquarters at Mercury House, by the Old Market Underpass, and I was one of the fourteen people accepted for the course. Two of those fourteen dropped out, and twelve of us completed and passed the course, only to be told that there were no suitable jobs for us! Two of the twelve were willing to wait. The rest of us accepted a 'bronze handshake' (payoff) and left. My three years with the Post Office were an amazing experience. The whole mentality and ethos was still 'Civil Service', as 90% of the staff had been. Whitleyism (trade unions), dead man's shoes, Bugginses turn, prevailed. Intractable case files were LITERALLY put under the carpet (to be found when the Senior Officer retired). It can all be summed up in the classic footnote of a Postmaster-General, who used to write on EVERY item, "For the appropriate action by the appropriate officer". Just how laid-back can one get?

My three years at Mercury House were more fruitful in other ways. I was only a few hundred yards from Bristol Arts Centre, where I was Director of Literature (till it closed in 1981). I was only a few hundred yards from the great Bristol newspaper building, where my friend Mike Lord was helping me promote poetry. I was only a few hundred yards from Colston House, where two arts officers were also keen to use poetry in the life of the City and County. In both time and place everything was coming together in great progress for poetry. It was the start of my busiest poetic decade. In 1970 I had my first bestseller poetry book. Six years before, my fourth poetry book *Wheel and Woe* had related only to cycling matters, and had taken five years to sell 5,000 copies. By 1970 I had hundreds of unused poems, of which twenty or thirty were good, and a hundred publishable. Very early in 1970 my dear father died, at home and in his sleep. He was only 79 and I was only 39, but he was a great influence upon my life. I was more than bereaved, something great had stopped. I designed the cover of my fifth poetry book, *All Systems Stop*, and selected the poems. It was a timely move, as I received an invitation to a Celebrity Poets Weekend in the Midlands, and I was one of the celebrity poets! It was a big event in the Orangery at Barton Seagrave house, and the organiser was the poet Nina Steane, who was also a painter, with works at the Royal Academy. Her husband was the headmaster of Kettering Grammar School, who tracked Russian space satellites much sooner than the American defences did. Red faces in the Pentagon. High-placed heads rolled. The first five thousand of my new book arrived on the same day as my invitation to Barton Seagrave. It was an omen. I took a thousand books to the reading and I sold the lot. The other 4,000 sold in a few months. A second, third, fourth, fifth, sixth and seventh 5,000 sold within three years, just in time for my 'annus mirabilis' of 1973. *All Systems Stop* had long-lasting lift off.

AT THE SCENE OF THE ACCIDENT – BRISTOL

Will anyone who saw the accident
Or can give any information,
Please communicate with God.

There were a few Romans with a few roads
A few monks with a Monastry
A few sailors with a few ships.

A few merchants
With an enviable reputation
For paying on the nail,
And hedging the everlasting bet
By building churches,
Outward and visible signs
Of inward and spiritual disgrace.

There was division of labour.
While St. Mary was on the Quay
St. Michael was on the Mount – Without.

Without what?
Without walls, said Cromwell,
And broke them down,
As he broke King Charles's neck.

But Bristol had the last word.
The merchants built their mansions
On the down. Whose down?
Kings Down.

And so the accident spread
Like blood and petrol on a motorway,
Coal to the East and Culture to the West.

Until Whitfield wooed Wesley to Wine Street,
And pushed him to preach at St. Philip's Marsh.
For the hearts of poor and rich – strangely warming.
Bristol, England, nor the World, his parish,
Were ever the same again. A new beginning
From a New Room. At Broadmead.

A city of many conveniences, public and otherwise.
Conveniently coloured people to trade in,
Conveniently sweet-burning weed
NICOTIANA TABACUM
To soothe the nerves of a nation
And endow monumental monstrosities.

Schools – for Chatterton to cheat at,
For Haig to happen at
For Iris Murdoch to mature at.

A bridge – for people to jump over,
A suburb for Betjeman to bumble over,
A theatre rescued from a rubbish heap.

Students and aeroplanes, both trying their wings.
Who can say which cost more?
Or which make more noise?

Accidents have inescapable attraction.
So has Bristol – for there are now
Half a million people
At the scene of the accident.

14

For Art's Sake

My three years at Mercury House had enabled me to focus on three aspects of poetry near to where I worked. I could go straight from work to the Bristol Arts Centre for many more events and group readings. I could go to Colston House in my lunch hour to see the City arts advisers, and plan more public events. I could use other lunch hours to discuss more newspaper poetry and *Evening Post*-sponsored events. Mike Lord was always helpful. He and his wife Alix now live at The Lizard, Cornwall, and protect owls and choughs from decline. They were recently doing that on BBC2 T.V. 'Coast'. My main concern, certainly until 1981, was the poetry and other literature at Bristol Arts Centre, 4 & 5 King Square, two large Georgian houses adapted to serve all the Arts, including films. I had been invited by the original founders of the Arts Centre to be Director of Literature. It was an honorary post, but there was a budget for many events. For nearly twenty years I averaged three sessions a week at the Arts Centre, about 3,000 sessions in all. The heart of the work was the Wednesday evening 'Circle In The Square' poetry meeting, which only had 120 members at any one time, but had thousands during the nineteen years. I also did regular Monday and Saturday sessions with poetry and other literature. By the early 1970s we were producing 1,000 poetry magazines in spring and autumn, which went all over Britain and abroad, including Scandinavia, France, Austria and the U.S.A. New York libraries bought a 100 copies each year, and copies were at Grand Central Station. There is a New York multi-arts centre called The Circle In The Square, and when Joanne Woodward (wife of Paul Newman) played the name part in *Candida* by George Bernard Shaw, I wrote to her at The Circle In The Square Theatre and had a pleasant reply. When I was teenage I played Marshbanks, the young poet who falls in love with Candida, the vicar's wife.

In all, our Circle In The Square publications totalled 28,000, the last ones being in 1976. We were also able to have a steady stream of distinguished guest poets throughout the 1960s and 1970s, even some from America, Europe and Russia. British Poets who came to us did so under a brilliant Arts Council arrangement run by the National Poetry Secretariat from Poetry Society head-quarters at 21 Earls Court Square, London, a former home-from-home to me. The N.P.S. ran a 'guarantee against loss' scheme, organised by Pamela Clunies-Ross. It meant that small promoters of poetry could hire major poets on a 'fee and expenses' basis, and know that all costs were covered. It provided us with many wonderful poetry events on weekday evenings and weekends. Bristol Central Library (and several branch libraries) were active in promoting poetry, and as recently as 2004 I have done a major event there, when it reopened after improvements. My main poetry connection with the Central Library was for six months in 1972/3, when I was asked to edit *600 Years of Bristol Poetry*, for the great festival celebrating 600 years of Bristol's Royal Charter. No expense was spared, and I had use of an office in the Library and the assistance of four gap-year senior scholars of the Cathedral School nearby. They were organised by their English teacher, Mr. Martin.

They sifted through 2,000 books and put markers for every poem I should look at. The city printer, about to retire, made the festival book his last task. It was also the last superb letter-press publication that they did, before cheaper, modern methods took over. Each thousand books had a different marbled cover with white spine and gold lettering. The Queen's copy was bound in red morocco leather, and gold embossed. Sir Bernard Lovell's copy (he was Patron of the Festival) was in blue morocco leather, and all Bristol councillors and chief officers had copies bound in blue calf leather. The public copies, with their glorious marbled designs, are now collectors' items, and hard to get. The festival also had a poetry competition and an invitation prize evening reading at the Little Theatre, Colston Hall. It was the first of many evenings that I was able to promote poetry at that lovely little theatre, now swallowed up in the bar lounge of the Colston Hall. All publicity, staffing, ticketing and artists' budget was fully covered by the City of Bristol. Bristol's great generosity led them to give The Circle In The Square a superb civic reception for our 1,000th meeting in June 1984, with speeches and readings. It was held at St. Nicholas Church Museum for 200 people.

At the time of our civic reception, John Betjeman had been dead one month. The weekend of 19th/20th May 1984 was very busy for me. Betjeman died about breakfast time on the Saturday of the Football Cup Final. I had to forget any idea of watching the match. From 10am onward, my telephone hardly stopped ringing. Journalists of national and provincial newspapers wanted much information about John Betjeman and his life. The detailed stuff. Some of the telephone calls lasted twenty minutes. I was glad it was not on my telephone bill. Several editors of West Country newspapers and magazines commissioned articles on Sir John, and one asked me to collaborate in a small memorial booklet of his life and works. I have since done that subject as a college course (several times), as a residential weekend course (at Urchfont Manor) and as two- or three-hour events at about twenty literary societies. In 2006 I did many events for his centenary. There was also a memorial service at St. Mary Redcliffe Church, Bristol, packed to the doors, and with famous readers. In the 1996 Poets' Corner Ceremony for John Betjeman the readers were Kenneth Cranham and Joanna Lumley, both of them excellent. It was a great event.

Lady Mary Wilson (Harold Wilson's widow) unveiled the memorial, and chaired a gala evening at King's College, London. She and John were poetic friends for many years. He died at his cottage 'Treen', Daymer Lane, Trebetherick, Cornwall, which he had bought for £8,000 without telling his wife Penelope about it. Poetic licence? Years later, I spent a day at 'Treen' when it was a holiday let.

Back to the 1970s! In 1972, before I did the *600 Years of Bristol Poetry*, I had a book published by Howard Sergeant (of OUTPOSTS

Magazine). It was called *Hardware and Software*, after my poem about the problems of computerisation. I am very doubtful of modern technology and global information. Not quite as doubtful as those who see all info-technology as 'The Mark of The Beast' in the biblical book of *Revelation*. Not quite, but almost. Because the little book of poems was superbly produced, I only had 1,000 copies of it, and sold them within six months, leaving me free to concentrate on the Bristol Festival book. I never knew how many copies of the *600 Years* book were printed. They were superb and expensive, but it was not my problem. They were a product of the City and County, and paid for by them. There were few of my works in it, but six months of my lifetime given to it. It has some rare treasures, including the only poems written by Iris Murdoch. So she said, when she gave permission to use them. She wrote them when she was a schoolgirl at Badminton School, Westbury-on-Trym, Bristol. The only other world famous girl from that school (that I know of) was Indira Gandhi of India.

I was able to get many copies of *600 Years of Bristol Poetry* for students and staff at Redland College when I started there. That meant that the principal, the head porter and myself were the best known people at the College (like the famous joke about Harry Bannister and the Pope on the Vatican balcony "I don't know who is the little man in White Robes, but the other one is Harry Bannister"). I even used to get stopped in Bristol streets to sign copies of the Festival book.

Throughout the 1970s Bristol Arts Centre was at its peak. Who could have guessed that by 1981 it would be closed and gone, and all its assets transferred to Watershed, to which I gave its name. The main problem was that one cannot run any theatre/cinema of 120 seats and make a balance, let alone a profit. The size of the theatre was dictated by available space, but several stupidities due to human decisions contributed to the decline of the Arts Centre. For at least ten years there was an annual subscription just to be a member. That was very sensible, bearing in mind that many people had put many thousands of pounds into founding the Arts

Centre. I guess that Billy and Jean Poeton put £20,000 of their own money into the foundation.

I never heard anybody object to a subscription of a few pounds a year before one started buying tickets. But the curse of the late century was creeping like mist from America, across the world of art (and eventually everything else). The poison of political correctness was on the march, trumpeted by the American feminist movement. Everything had to have an 'ISM' and an 'IST'. All 'highest common factors' had to become 'lowest common denominators' (so that no loser could be offended). Bold bright posters had to become trendily turgid, and, by 1980, brown print on brown paper. Verily, I kid you not.

Annual subscriptions were abolished, all pre-payments were abolished, and all non-theatre events had derisory charges. Few understood why, but it was an early sign that nobody's human rights must be abused by asking them to pay for anything. More events were done at outside venues, in the gardens, in College Green, or on the streets of Bristol. This was to avoid oppressing the public with the idea that they had to attend indoors, or concentrate or participate in anything. To ask anything of anybody was to infringe human rights. Auto-destructive art was in the gallery, auto-motive art was on the walls. It was too hard on poor put-upon people. They needed auto-matic art served up on a plate, in their own homes, at their own times, Boo, Hoo! All this was heartbreaking to those of us who had over fifteen years of providing rigorous quality drama (including some world premières), films from all the classic genres, music of high standard, and literature, ancient and modern, of quality.

Most of the founder-directors had gone. Only John Bedford and I remained all the time. Most of the top-class performers had gone (the early dramas were better than provincial repertory standards). All the great social life of the Arts Centre had gone. Two full-time staff, Reg Allsop and Sonia Price, did an heroic job of keeping the Arts Centre open, but it was to prove too little, too late. The great empty warehouse that was to become Watershed, by the Docks, was already holding auction sales to raise awareness of the future venture. The ultimate aim was carefully concealed from the stalwarts of the old regime. The wonderful old wardrobe mistress was bewildered to see all her years of hard work devalued, till the Saturday morning when it was all put out on the pavement in the rain. In the last year a professional arts organiser was brought in (from New Zealand, God help us) to rearrange the deckchairs on the ship. It was classic closure, smooth, silent and subterranean. Go into a dark room, and see what develops. A new picture develops from a negative. Develops? Ah, yes, developers. The Gods of Latter Days. The whole emphasis and effort moved to Watershed. That media centre, by Bristol Centre, by the Docks, and by sponsorship from High Places, has become an international focus for techno-media. Most of the many arts it ignores.

AN OLD PROFESSOR LOOKS BACK

Strange that, when young, I was regarded
Despite high marks, as a "clever clod";
But I won the prizes which were awarded,
And I quickly learned, "Who awards is God".

Based on that predatory awareness
I built my swoop and snatch career.
Students (but what are they) despised me;
My masters, flattered, held me dear.

They were the focus of my planning;
Sycophant I of their small sect,
Knowing that every past praise counted
When there was someone to elect.

And, when I wrote, I wrote discreetly
For the few hundred with the Power,
Putting on paper That precisely
Which they were wanting at that hour.

Powers change, and hours change. I did also,
Learning to sense the coming thing –
So that my soft Vicarious Braying
Ushered me in a Second Spring.

Third, Fourth and Fifth … they are past counting,
But I have come to learn of late,
Selling your psyche to the Devil
Means, Sell your birthright to the State.

Strangely, a Heart Disease afflicts me,
And, sometime soon, I have to die.
Grant me the time, the strength, to write one
Posthumous-published last Great Lie.

INQUISITION

The Holy Office
Has transferred its offices,
Its good offices,
To Moscow,
Thinking, as ever,
Only of its children's good,
Its children's eternal good,
For which their present suffering
Is payment in advance.

Lord have mercy.

Whom the Holy Office love
They chasten. Therefore
Do not question our love,
Our all-embracing love,
The embrace of the bear.

Alexander Ginsburg, heretic,
We love you
With years of suffering.

Yuri Galenskov, heretic,
We love you
With years of suffering.

Alexei Dobrovolsky, heretic,
We love you
With years of suffering.

Vera Lashkova, typist to heretics,
We love you
With a year's suffering

Lord have mercy.

15

Words, Words, Words

When Steven Spielberg telephoned Tom Stoppard to commission a film script for a Hollywood film, he was totally confident of success. When Stoppard declined to do it, because he was busy writing a script for the BBC, the stunned Spielberg made mocking scorn of a puny play for BBC Television. "Not television", said Stoppard, "for RADIO". (Complete collapse of Steven Spielberg.) But Tom Stoppard (whom I met when he was a very young journalist at Bristol) was right. The supreme scripts are all for radio. *Under Milk Wood*, by Dylan Thomas, is the greatest ever. Stoppard's own *Albert's Bridge* and *If you'll be Glad, I'll be Frank* make superb radio. The 'Toytown' radio scripts of my childhood are still vivid in my mind. I can still SEE (seventy years on) Larry the Lamb, Denis the Dachshund ("Larry, mein Freund"), Mr. Growser, Mr. Mayor and the others. No T.V. docuDrama will ever equal the *Mysterious Matter of The Arkville Coach*. Imagination is evoked merely by the name. Has any stage or screen portrayal of a Charles Dickens novel ever equalled the original book? I do not believe it has. I have never seen any portrayal of *Barnaby Rudge*, but the words give a picture of the man to the mind's eye. My six-year old granddaughter Jasmine has gone off illustrated books. She now writes and reads "Words only" books, which she calls 'imagination books'. She also loves The Dictionary. I suddenly realise that Sullivan is only the sidekick of W.S. Gilbert, and George Gershwin is ancillary to Ira Gershwin. Song music is to lubricate the words.

From early childhood the wonder of words has held me enthralled, sad, serious or funny. As soon as I could hold a pencil, I wrote little verses that rhymed, and I loved the rhythm of nursery rhymes. I collected books of poetry long before I went to school. Robert Louis Stevenson told me, "The world is so full of a number of things, I'm sure we should all be as happy as Kings". And I was. And I still am. I owe a deep debt to Auden and Arnold, Byron and Blake, Coleridge and Clare, Dryden and Donne, Eliot and Ewart, Fitzgerald and Flecker, Goldsmith and Gray, Herrick and Hood, Jean Ingelow, Ben Johnson, Keats and Kipling, Landor and Lovelace, Milton and Moore, Newbolt and Nash, Owen and O'Shaughnessy, Pope and Patmore, Francis Quarles, both the Rossettis, Shakespeare and Shelley, Tennyson and Thompson, U (who?), Vaughan and Verstegan, Wordsworth and Wyatt, X(cess), WB Yeats, Z, all said, and so to bed. Those were my rich sources before I was teenage, when I became a reader of modern poets. And all the time I was trying to repay my debt by writing poems of my own, a few a day. Mostly poor things, but mine own. The poor things are the practice for the good things. The most (quantity) spontaneous poems in one day were twenty seven, the most planned and prepared poems in one day were sixty six, in a style that I invented in 1986, The Glimmerick, the Limerick to cast light. After I attended the Bristol reading of U.A. Fanthorpe's *Selected Poems* (King Penguin Book, 66 poems) I invented a verse form with the rhyme scheme of a Limerick (aa bb a) and the line length of Shakespeare (iambic pentameters). Some of Ursula's poems were long, but I managed to encapsulate each poem in five lines of ten syllables, make all 66 into a book *Short Back and Side Effects*, and send it to Ursula for her amazement. It is a kindness that she still speaks to me. I particularly enjoy poetic compression. In 2004 I was asked to sum up one hundred years of my Old School Club in fifty lines, for a centenary celebration. I compressed 100 years into 48 lines, which went to every member and other interested people worldwide.

Since the 1960s, members and magazines of The Circle In The Square Poets have gone all over the world, and we have been associated with hundreds of other small magazines. It is time to consider some of those poetry links, and some of the poets who enriched our lives. I was aware that most of the C.I.T.S. Poets were sending their poems regularly to many magazines. It is something that I have never done, even when I respected the ability of the editors. My mood has always been so autonomous that I controlled the covers, the type-face, the paper weight and the layout of every page. I was mildly miffed that I could not control the black ink and the gauge of the staples. Freakish. But I never touched (to alter) another's work. If I accepted it, I accepted it exactly as they did it, 'warts and all'. The same applied to the hundred or more competitions I have judged. Only twelve of the competitions were run by myself, on behalf of North Somerset County, from 1991 to 2002. The total entries to those twelve competitions were about 4,000 poems, and I gave three money prizes each year, and a perpetual silver cup trophy, in memory of my father. Since 2003, that cup is annually awarded within Weston Youth Arts Festival. Apart from my own competitions, I part-judged (one of a final team) or pre-judged (to save some famous judges weeks of toil) whole competitions. My biggest task, about 50 years ago, was 8,000 scripts for the Cheltenham Festival of Literature, ten weeks toil for £1,000 reward (2/6d per script). I handed to three notable judges 500 scripts to be finally assessed. My 500 choices included every poem that had any possible merit, even in styles that I disliked. One must be objective and impartial! I have done that kind of judging about 90 times in 50 years. It usually takes several weeks. The only other poetry that I take time over is my fairly regular commissioned work, with every detail dictated by the customer. Most of my commissions are for sonnets, fourteen very specific lines for lovers, partners, Valentines and others. Often I write their sonnet while they wait, in about half an hour. What cost £5 from 1950 to 1971, and £10 from 1971 (new currency) to 2000, is now £20 for 14 lines. Some commissioned works are 30 or 40 lines long, and a few are 100 lines or more, for special occasions. Nowadays all my non-sonnets are £1 per line, very reasonable compared with commissions in other arts.

My personal poems take little effort. I always think of the ending first, one line, two lines or four. Then I work out a title which will guide the whole work. With startpoint and destination, the middle of the poem should almost write itself, once the choice of metrical rhythm and line-length have been made. Only a very long poem should take longer than an hour.

Other poets I have met have other methods, and lifestyles to suit their personalities. I had regular contact with the three Mersey Poets in their most famous years. They shared one of the twenty-seven volumes of 'Penguin Modern Poets', simply called *The Mersey Poets*. It is said that their volume sold as many copies as all the other twenty six volumes put together. Those three compared with 78 other poets? That is an exaggeration, but the Mersey Poets certainly sold far more copies than any of the other volumes. The only link of the three was Liverpool. They were young in the days of The Cavern and Beatlemania. In a sense, they were a spin off from Beatlemania, but they always had differing style and appearance. Adrian Henri, large and loud, had a visual arts background, a huge appetite for alcohol and women, and is the only one not still alive, to the surprise of very few. His collection of thrown panties was alleged to exceed that of any musical popstar. Brian Patten was the mystical one (and still is). His 'radar' created the illusion of going everywhere with his eyes closed. He was 'discovered' a second time by the publishers George Allen and Unwin who boosted his career. Of the three Mersey Poets, Patten may prove the most enduring in public memory, as his poems float like a butterfly and sting like a bee. Roger McGough was (and is) the most cerebral of the three, in literature and in life. His clever work picked its way through the minefields of decades, until he is now suburbanly smooth, and living at Barnes, by the river Thames, the suburb of all the arts. His books are everywhere, his broadcasts are everywhen, his influence is ubiquitous. One wonders whether he had it all planned fifty years ago, in Liverpool? But I can remember when they were doing small gigs with others, including myself. We read at Hotwells Chapel Arts Centre, we read at several Bristol and Somerset comprehensive schools, and a few colleges. They were heady days.

I can remember a big poetry reading I shared with Brian Patten at Trowbridge College. Or we would have shared it, if he had arrived. Times of arrival, and geographical locations were never Brian's strong points. His publishers were promoting a book called *The House That Jack Built*, with poems by Brian, myself and others. All profits went to SHELTER, the Housing Charity. Trowbridge College had a five-day exhibition (for Shelter) and on the final Friday we were to do three readings, two in the morning, one in the afternoon. I drove there an hour early. A van with 600 books arrived. He did not arrive. (It could have been a 'morning after the night before'. He had many of those mornings.) I did the first reading, and sold hundreds of books. I did the second reading, and sold hundreds of books. I did not know that I had sold all the books, including my own reading copy. To do the afternoon reading, I had to borrow a copy from a member of staff. Since then I have always cut the book-corners, front and back, off my reading copy, so that it can never get accidentally sold. The events were so successful that Brian blissfully got away with it.

I have shared readings (all over Britain) with almost all the published poets of the 1960s, 1970s and 1980s. I particularly enjoyed readings (several) with Charles Causley and one with Ian MacMillan, now (like Roger McGough) always on radio, T.V. and critical programmes. He is a great talent. Will there soon be a statue at Barnsley?

Radio reminds me of another great medium for poetry, perhaps THE medium for poetry. In 1969, I was advisory to a committee at Bristol planning to set up Radio Bristol BBC Station, at Tyndalls Park Road, alongside the main BBC building in Whiteladies Road. My unique knowledge of the local poetry scene was useful to them, and my reward was a series of twenty-five poetry programmes, each with a man and woman poet I chose from the Bristol area. Fifty poets got their first broadcasts in 1970. All the now-famous presenters were new beginners, even a girl called Kate Adie and a lad called John Turner. The late Roger Bennett was another. Peter Robins, the London BBC man who had chaired the planning committee of Radio Bristol, was putting together a poetry book for CORGI Transworld. It was a mass-market paperback with all the current name poets, including poems by me. It was launched on New Year's Eve 1969/1970, called *Doves for the Seventies* at the Queen Elizabeth Hall on London's South Bank. All the seats and all the copies that night sold, and hundreds of thousands more in 1970/74. Julie Felix did the song and guitar music for the event, and a dozen of us read our works till New Year. As I left the hall, into the cold damp night, I thought back fifteen, sixteen, seventeen, eighteen, nineteen years to turning out of the Albert Hall, after the Chelsea Arts Balls, and walking to Covent Garden for a soup-and-bread breakfast. Happy days.

Another great platform for poetry is anthologies. Just as *Palgrave's Golden Treasury* is still selling in its third century, so do other anthologies promote the poems of thousands. In 1982 Redcliffe Press published a 94-poem book of my favourite poems, called *Loosing My Grip*, and those poems have now gone all over the English-speaking world. An earlier book of my poems (with a title chosen by Professor Christopher Ricks) called *Everything By Starts*, had also gone worldwide. Christopher Ricks had seven years as Professor of English at Bristol University, and often came to Circle In The Square meetings. He thought I was like the eccentric Duke of Buckingham, described by John Dryden in 'Absolom and Achitophel' as being "everything by starts, and nothing long". So that became the title of another of my books. The house of Christopher Ricks was on a corner in Clifton, opposite a small picture gallery called Arnolfini. That small venture has now become a large arts complex on the Bristol dockside, noted for its very wide-ranging artistic policies. In its very early days I did poetry readings at Arnolfini, including one event lasting a whole weekend. In the 1960s, 1970s and 1980s I also did readings in a dozen Bristol pubs that were popular places for poetry. An actress and I read the whole *Rubaiyat of Omar Khayyam* at Bristol Old Vic Theatre.

Perhaps the most popular outlets for poetry are small magazines. They are so flexible, variable and inexpensive that they can function almost anywhere. I edited 28 editions of *Circle In The Square*, each of 1,000 copies, from 1966 to 1976. Any small magazine depends upon its editor, and most editors (but not all) are poets, or have been poets. My magazine lasted a decade. Some poetry magazines have lasted five decades, but those tend to become full-time enterprises. Some die with their first editor, others take on new life with a new editor. The magazine OUTPOSTS was founded in 1944 (in wartime) by Howard Sergeant, and he edited more than 100 issues before he died. I still remember the major reading for OUTPOSTS 100 at the Mermaid Theatre, Puddle Dock, City of London. It was a big event, hosted by Howard himself and Kingsley Amis, a fine poet as well as a best-selling novelist. Poets travelled from all over Britain to celebrate 100 issues of the magazine. Hundreds of well known poets were there, some of them OUTPOSTS discoveries. I was sitting next to the famous Welsh poet, Alison Bielski, who lived and worked in many Welsh locations. She was also a distinguished visual artist and a talented musician on traditional keyboard instruments and the Welsh harp. Her poetry ranged from modern pictorial to traditional iambic. She had a particular gift for sonnets, and published a whole book of them. She also wrote prose works. OUTPOSTS magazine went on to 180 issues under the editorship of Roland John. The best of the present long-lived magazines is ACUMEN, edited at Brixham in Devon by Patricia Oxley, whose husband William is also a poet and prose author. He had a famous radical poetry and critical magazine called 'LITTACK' (self explanatory). Its fiery combustion burned out. Patricia's patient editorship has created an exemplary literary journal, now at 57 issues and ongoing. It is very good value.

The British Little Magazine Scene attracted the interest of an English Professor at Salzburg University, Austria. Professor James Hogg, whom I met on one of my many visits to Austria, may have wanted to restore the balance to the 'Sound of Words', after

123

The Sound of Music (a famous film of nuns and Nazis) became the world image of Salzburg. One of James Hogg's learned assistants at the Institut für Anglistik und Amerikanistik, Wolfgang Görtschacher, has done a massive study (750 pages) of British LITTLE MAGAZINE PROFILES (1939–1993). It is a wonderful work of scholarship, and also a living account, with interviews, of the English poetry world in the 54 years studied. He sees the need for an editor to be a "manic obsessive". Two of his examples are myself and Fred Beake (long-time member of The Circle In The Square Poets, while also editor of *The Poet's Voice*). For ten years and twenty eight issues I produced the *Circle In The Square* magazine entirely solo. An American survey of 160 small literary magazines revealed that 38 were worked by one person, 36 by two people, 22 by three, 15 by four, 12 by five people, and the remaining 37 by six or more people. Paradoxically, the large team is physically easier, and otherwise harder. Creative committees tend to produce camels and giraffes. Görtschacher's analyses of the decade 1940 to 1950, 1951 to 1958, 1959 to 1977, 1978 to 1985 and 1986 to 1993 are splendid short surveys. His next 240 pages are case study interviews with editors, critics, poets and one librarian, Geoffrey Soar, The Librarian of Little Magazines. Many city libraries and university libraries in Britain, France, Scandinavia, U.S.A, and Commonwealth countries subscribed to my *Circle In The Square* magazine from 1966 to 1976. Görtschacher mentions *Circle In The Square* five times and myself three times. He also mentions (for their connection with our group) Fred Beake, Jenny Johnson, Wes Magee, Charles Hobday, Ryl Lovell, Abe Adams, Alison Bielski, and Chris Hunt and Liz Lochhead, a famous Glasgow author who was occasionally with us. Liz Lochhead is also a noted playwright, and two of the C.I.T.S. poets became BBC Radio playwrights, Melissa Murray and Elaine Eveleigh, a verbal genius. Such a talented tally from one poetry group at Bristol.

On the national editorial stage, Görtschacher interviewed Roland John, second editor of OUTPOSTS, after Howard Sergeant died. He also interviewed Peter Dale, editor of AGENDA and Michael Horovitz of NEW DEPARTURES, who wrote *Children of Albion* and other significant works. His ex-wife Frances Horovitz was a major poet who died young, and we gave her a massive memorial reading at the Colston Hall, Bristol. It was the last time I had a conversation with Ted Hughes before he died. Another poetry editor that Görtschacher interviewed was Mike Shields of ORBIS, an Industry researcher and Scientist (and translator in ten languages). Many Editors are from non-Arts backgrounds. William Oxley (LITTACK, LITTACK SUPPLEMENT and NEW HEADLAND) was an Accountant, and is the husband of excellent editor, Patricia Oxley (ACUMEN). Michael Schmidt (PN Review) is nowadays Carcanet Press, and an academic and broadcaster. He has edited very many English and British poetry books. Another major academic interviewed was Kathleen Raine (TEMENOS); originally a scientist, she has won many literary awards.

During the nineteen years of Bristol Arts Centre, I was often interviewed by graduates researching Circle In The Square for Master's or PhDs of the Sorbonne (Paris), various American Universities, and by a teaching nun who was doing a Master's Degree at Warwick University. I was also interviewed by many journalists from very varied publications about the poets and publications of Circle In The Square. One of our poets, Diana Hendry, became a major author and won one of the Whitbread prizes. She now lives in Scotland, and I find her poems in POETRY SCOTLAND to this day. I will be reading at their annual September Festival, in Callander, this year (2007).

Perhaps the most personal poetry has been written ABOUT myself, by others. There have been scores of sonnets, and over a hundred personal poems in total. Almost all were favourable, and almost all were by women. Knowing that I cannot write any villanelles, one well known woman poet has written a powerful villanelle about me. The perfect game, set and match. About twenty of the personal poems are in the public domain. All the others are totally treasured by the author's privacy. Quite apart from poems about me by others, I have figured in three plays (that I know of) and two novels by famous authors, one novel filmed with a famous cast. The only clue to that is eponymous. The other novel is the last novel by Muriel Spark. She stored my teenage character for almost sixty years before writing about it just before she died.

Until I wrote this book, I would have regarded, and do regard, my poetry (about any subject) as my autobiography. It's all there if you search. My 1997 book *Half a Ton: Selected Poems 1947–1997*, has about 200 poems and prose essays. Almost every page can be rich in revelations. As was said of Sir Christopher Wren and St. Paul's Cathedral: SI MONUMENTUM REQUIRIS CIRCUMSPICE. If you seek a monument, look around.

HARDWARE AND SOFTWARE

There remain these three –
Hardware,
Software,
And electricity.
And the greatest of these
Is electricity.

But they cut off
My electricity.

Though I talk
With the tongues
Of men and of angels
And have not
Hardware, software
And electricity,
I am become as
A snorting pig
Or a grunting barbarian.

But they have cut off
My electricity.
And my hardware
Burns with coldness.
And my software
Rots with damp.

NIGHT AND DAY

I cannot help if I find the day
Insipid by comparison with night;
It surely is my uncontested right
To see life in the way that is my way?

I see it as a parallel to thoughts
That dressed stone buildings are superior rocks,
That Art and Craft and artefact unlocks
Whole worlds beyond crude Nature's dull resorts.

Therefore I shall continue to be glad
Good furniture's superior to trees,
And woollen cloth is likelier to please
Than overheated sheep, all sweating mad.

Day is the guardian of all Nature's blind;
Night calls for special eyes to see
And special skills to fashion and set free
Contrivance from the crudities we find.

When next the sunlight fades and day grows dim
Remember, some folks like the world that way –
When light of lamps (as light of mind would say)
Sings real illumination as its hymn.

16

Go West, Young Man

"Going West" used to be a phrase for ruin, downfall or demise. But not in my life, where it has meant the exact opposite, as it did in the U.S.A. in the 19th century. If you wanted space, freedom, autonomy, go west. Seamus Heaney's famous poem 'Bogland' is an awareness of that, granted him during his time teaching in California. "We have no prairies" (in his homeland, Ireland). His homeland has depth without direction; America has direction without depth. Seamus was a friend of our head of English at Redland College, Eddie Wainwright, whose ex-wife Verena (a Viennese) was one of my colleagues during all my years at Stoke Lodge Adult Education Centre, Bristol. Verena used to organise annual coach holidays in Austria and Bavaria, wonderful fortnights of culture. Eddie Wainwright used to get Seamus Heaney to Redland College to give us occasional lectures, always full of interest and insight. I saw the early years of Heaney's infiltration into Scandinavia (with only the most Nobel intentions). It worked so well that The Prize was richly deserved.

I first followed the command "Go West" in 1956, to become a theological student for three years, and to find a wonderful wife. From 1959 to 1963 I was 'back East', in London and Essex, but from 1964 to date I have been a Bristol and Somerset man, with many links to Cornwall, Devon, Dorset and Gloucestershire. Those 43 years have been blessed in many ways. The West has opened dozens of doors to me, and enabled me to be several different people, each moderately successful. Perfect Provincialism. One of my regular Bristol poets in the 1960s and 1970s was Geraldine Kaye, also a gifted author of novels for young people. She was a leading member of the West Country Writers Association, founded in 1951 by Waveney Girvan "to foster, by the interchange of ideas, the love of literature in the West

Country". Waveney Girvan was a Scot, who had lived wherever his father's military postings took him. One of those postings was Bodmin, and young Waveney loved it. (Thinks: If you can love Bodmin you can love anywhere.) In adult years he was an honorary Cornishman. A high percentage of 'West Country Writers' originated elsewhere, most famously Daphne du Maurier, of the many novels. She was a French Londoner, as indeed am I also. A French Londoner with four Yorkshire grandparents (me).

Every year, early in May, the West Country Writers have a weekend congress (nothing naughty) in a different town or city, from Penzance to Worcester, from Weston-super-Mare to Salisbury. By 1970, I had five published books, including one that sold 35,000 copies (*All Systems Stop* 1970). In 1971 Geraldine Kaye (a Circle In The Square poet) put me forward for Membership of 'West Country Writers' and I was approved, as a suitable case for treatment. Any member prepared to gamble on living another ten years can pay ten times the annual subscription, and be a life member. My ten subs. have covered 36 years, so far. The 1971 Congress was at Torquay, but Fawlty Towers was too small to take our members, so we met at a larger hotel, with a sane manager. Our guest of honour was Agatha Christie, a local lady who had written a few crime novels, and a popular play *The Mousetrap*. She gave a splendidly forensic talk, but did not use her knife and fork for any medical matters. My months of May are very busy, so it was in 1973 before I again met all the congress attenders, usually 100 members, plus partners and guests. I was gradually making friends, and discovering that poets were few among those prosaic persons. In 1973 we met at Exeter, and our guest of honour was Jennie Lee (Minister of Arts), Aneurin Bevan's widow (Baroness of Asheridge). Exeter was a city I knew well, as I was very active in South West Arts in that city and university. I was able to show some writers the wonders of South West Arts headquarters. My next WCWA Congress was in 1976, at Bristol. In years ending in '6' we usually met at Bristol, at the

Royal Hotel by College Green, a luxury experience, but usually too hot. I once asked the housekeeper why was it so expensively heated, when WCWA could provide all the hot air?

In 56 years the WCWA has only had four Presidents, a remarkable record. The first was Eden Philpotts (Mr. Devon) a wonderful writer of country fact, fiction and drama. His books evoke a lost world of rural delight. He served from 1951 to 1960, and was followed by Henry Williamson, famous nature novelist (*Tarka the Otter* etc.) and person novelist, and controversialist. He served five years, and was succeeded by Christopher Fry, a poet and poetic dramatist whose mastery of verse drama is amongst the greatest. I have all his plays, and have seen several staged. Even Margaret Thatcher steals his titles, "The Lady's not for turning" (burning). Christopher angered the young Richard Burton, by taking him out of that famous play in London's West End, and sending him to a small play in Hammersmith. Burton protested as though Hammersmith (The Lyric), were a tented production in Outer Mongolia! Was that the ONLY occasion anyone ever confronted Burton? Christopher Fry's presidency reached almost forty years, just as he reached almost a hundred years. His intelligence, charm and wit lasted to the end. I know, because I was often the butt of his wit. His home area, East Dene, Chichester, Sussex, is the heart of the area covered by H.G. Wells' enchanting novel *The Wheels of Chance*, about a lady cyclist pursued by various good and bad male cyclists. That novel belongs with *Kipps* ('Half a Sixpence') and *The History of Mr. Polly* as a unique trilogy of Edwardian social comment and good fun. The fourth and present president of WCWA is Lady Rachel Billington, a very varied author, reviewer and feature writer, who has also written BBC radio and television plays and several books for children. We wish her a long and influential time as President of West Country Writers Association.

My next experience at WCWA Congress was at Exeter in 1980, and our guest speaker was the famous *Marnie* and *Poldark* novelist Winston Graham. Another speaker that year was Frank Delaney.

131

Like the membership, our guests cover a wide range of authorship. Winston Graham's works had brilliant television series, all Cornwall-based. His *Marnie* was a powerful Hollywood film by Alfred Hitchcock. It had Sean Connery, Tippi Hedren and the young Bruce Dern (1964). In 1982 WCWA met at Cheltenham and I heard Penelope Lively give the main talk. Her powerful novels (and children's books which preceded them) have won many prizes, and her collected short stories are still popular. Her autobiography *Oleander, Jacaranda* was published in 1994. In 1983, I attended my sixth WCWA Weekend at Taunton, where the County Hotel was a very suitable venue. After twelve years in WCWA, I knew many writers, and the Sunday coincided with the bi-centenary of the *Observer* newspaper. Before breakfast on the Sunday, the new chairman, Anthony Hippisley Coxe (founder of the Theatre Museum in London) and myself went on a tour of newsagents, and bought dozens of *Observers* so that all who wanted one could have one. My interest in literary ephemera causes me to collect, and I have tens of thousands of literary ephemera. In the following year 1984, I was newsletter editor for WCWA, in a year when the constitution was being revised. Because of the extra information, I changed the format to A4 (twice as large) but my successor soon changed it back to pocket-book size. I assume that members carry their newsletters everywhere. We were at Torquay in 1984, and a computer company provided an exhibition and advice on computers. That was 23 years ago, and I have still never touched a key of a computer. My elder daughter does such modern matters for me, if necessary. My younger daughter leaves all her book details to the professionals who produce her glossy books about cakes and cake decoration. She also is a life member of West Country Writers, but is too busy in May to attend.

In 1985, WCWA met at Weston-super-Mare (the only year that it has done so) and Laurie Lee and his wife were there. Laurie had a special regard for Weston, as one chapter of *Cider With Rosie*, about the Slad Parish Outing (by Charabanc) indicates. I had a long walk with him and his wife, almost to Uphill and back. Before *Cider With Rosie* (1959) Laurie was mainly a poet and scriptwriter. But his masterwork, followed by his second volume of autobiography, and a third in 1991 have caused the public to forget that he was first a poet. He gave me a copy of his poetry book *My Many-Coated Man*, inscribed 'To Bill Pickard, with admiration'. It is one of my treasures. I read with Laurie twice, once in a pub and once in an orchard at night, with lanterns hung from the branches. Hundreds attended, and it was a very atmospheric reading. In 1987 WCWA met at Weymouth and in 1989 at Barnstaple, my tenth May Congress. Barnstaple is a charming town and a good centre. The cycleway along the riverside goes to Instow, Bideford and Torrington, where the railway station has been made into a pub, called The Puffing Billy. I bicycled there, and I have the t-shirt. Across the river are Westward Ho! and Appledore, teenage haunts of Rudyard Kipling in the 1880s.

My May Weekend in 1992 was very special. It was at Penzance, and I was invited to give a verse eulogy to the town and district. I drew a civic shield (with choughs) and wrote the verses on the other side of the shield. I understand it is in the Penzance archives. In 1994 we were again at Cheltenham, and the Guest Speaker was Diana Hendry (one of my Circle In The Square poets) who won the Whitbread Prize for one of her prose works. In 1996 we were again at the Royal Hotel at Bristol, and John Mortimer, playwright and creator of *Rumpole of the Bailey*, was our guest speaker. He had distinguished back-up, as the other speakers were Melvyn Bragg, Deborah Moggach and Christopher Fry. In 1998, my fourteenth WCWA Congress (in 27 years) was at Weymouth again, and Margaret Drabble was our guest speaker. She graces many branches of literature, novels, massive works of reference, and many lesser works. She had moved to Porlock, in the West Country, but still had her main home in London, with her husband Michael Holroyd, the notable biographer. Many years earlier Margaret and I had met at Bristol Arts Centre, when she used to do events such as reading from unpublished manuscripts (which we later saw as best selling novels). During her foreign travels, she always sent me postcards from exotic places, and unusual gifts, often related to me being a Piscean. Since 1998, my time in May has been too busy to attend WCWA, but I hope to manage May 2008, when they are again at Bristol, but not at the (globally warmed) Royal Hotel.

My 36 years (so far) in the West Country Writers have given me contact with an amazing assortment of interesting people, a great contrast with the essential loneliness of being a writer. A poet can cure that by readings in hundreds of places throughout Britain and beyond. In the West Country I have read at dozens of different towns and cities, in famous company such as Charles Causley, or in unknown company. My regular reading places were Bristol, Bath, Swindon, Clevedon, Weston, and also Newport and Cardiff in Wales, very West!

I have life membership of the fairly new Charles Causley Society (Launceston), and the Jane Austen Society, as far east as Hampshire, with much activity at Bath. Since the 1980s I have had much contact, and done many events, with the John Betjeman Society, ranging from Canterbury in the east, to London, to Wiltshire, to Bath and Bristol, and in Cornwall, around Trebetherick, where John is buried. Just as the West Country was a rich source of inspiration to Betjeman, so it has been to me. The West Country has given me ten years of full-time adult study; it has given me hundreds of literary colleagues, from Cornwall to Cheltenham, and from the Welsh borders to Wiltshire, but Causley, Laurie Lee and Betjeman hold special places in my memory.

One of Betjeman's 2006 centenary events was when Pam Ayres, another poetry friend, read her own special poem at his former home in the Vale of The White Horse. Pam's childhood was in that area, and she warmly evoked the memories it had for her and John.

HIBERNATION

A belly full,
A warm bed,
And a long sleep.

What more can be said
About those months
In limbo.

There comes a day
In Autumn
When all reason cries
Counterfeit death
Before the last rose dies.

Counterfeit death
Until the season bring
Not roses
But the humbler flowers
Of Spring.

Then blink your eyes,
Stretch, swear,
And move about.
Summer demands
Your counterfeit of life.

Savour the flowers.
The fruits and nuts will keep
Until it's time again
For a belly full,
A warm bed,
And a long sleep.

SANCTIONS

Everyone, at some time,
Contemplates a Unilateral
Declaration of Independence.
And the world's answer
Is sanctions.

Because of the sanctions
Some give up the idea
Before they are weaned.
Others, when they go to school.
Most succumb at school leaving.

And they promise themselves
That at sixty-five,
Or even sixty –
Hallelujah, even sixty –
They will make their declaration.

But long before then
Sanctions become reasons,
And reasons become excuses,
And excuses become habits,
And habits become chains.

And cutting off chains
Is a process
Painful
To the wrists
And the ankles.

It is rocking-chair rumination
That although our lives
May not have been lived,
Our existences
Have been sanctioned.

17

Education, Education, Education

I have never met Prime Minister Tony Blair, but he should view me as a living example of his great priorities, "Education, Education, Education". My parents shared those priorities, and got me used to real reading and simple study from age one year to age five (four beads on the abacus). From September 1936 to September 1939 I was at Salters Hill L.C.C. Primary School (three beads on the abacus). From 1939 to 1942 I was at a Private School near Leatherhead, Surrey (three beads on the abacus). From 1942 to 1947 I was at Mercers' School, Holborn, London (five beads on the abacus). From 1947 to 1949 and from 1951 to 1956 I had seven years commercial education, UK and Export (seven beads on the abacus), and from 1949 to 1951 I had two years military education (two beads on the abacus). From 1956 to 1959 I had three years theological studies at Bristol (three beads on the abacus). To get to Bristol I had done five years correspondence studies for Higher School Certificates, and in 1957 to 1959 I worked three summers in the London parks and three Decembers on the parcel post, rich studies in practical experience. From 1959 to 1968 I had nine years in the School of Life and Hard Knocks, before three years of study for Institute of Personnel Management (three beads on the abacus), in the years 1969 to 1972. So, by 41 years of age, I had 30 years of education.

That was not enough. In 1973 I was invited to join the Bachelor of Education Course (main: Religious Studies) at Redland College, Bristol, now part of the University of the West of England. It was a four-year course, with side subjects Theory of Education, English, Maths, and Geography. That course boosted the beads on the abacus to 34 years. At 46 years of age (1977) I had only 12 years that were 'general' years, 19 years if I include Tate & Lyle. Certainly, 27 years were formally educational. In some ways

137

my four years at Redland College were the most interesting and varied of them all. The variety and interest of the staff and my fellow students were remarkably great. Many were mature students, some even older than myself, who had completed careers. One had been a police inspector, another a farmer and author. Several had been self-employed and wanted to teach others their expertise. Not only educationally, but socially, it was a great melting pot, always on the boil. The *News of The World* banner boast "All Human life" was certainly there. My head of department, a Methodist professor, had ten university degrees, four of them in science, and was the most educated man that I have ever met. Some of the R.E. staff were less qualified than myself, but they were all interesting. Each of the students chose a subject for a long dissertation, to be compiled over three or four years. I chose 'War and Peace in the Holy Bible'. My dissertation was as long as this book, and had 84 different books in its bibliography. It was read by a Bristol University theologian who marked it A+ plus.

I started at the College fresh from the Bristol 600 Years Festival, and spent the first three months being asked to sign books that I had edited. The requests continued well in to 1974, and occasionally 1975. I found the theological part of my studies very easy compared with previous religious studies, and English, Mathematics and Geography were quite straightforward. Educational Theory was quite the reverse of straightforward. It was quite acceptable to learn all different ideas about Education; it was not acceptable to be taught that any particular one or two of them were 'flavour of the decade' and must be promoted. Every decade has had its fashionable flavour, and much misery it has caused to teachers and pupils. One of my tutors asserted that "History began in 1844" (with Karl Marx). He was an active Communist and probably still is. One of the tutors in educational philosophy ruled out all ideas except his own ideas, and marked all our work on that basis. NOT a truly philosophical approach.

Against academic argument, there was plenty of light relief. I organised a large 'Old Time Music Hall', attended by many hundreds of staff and students. Many very talented acts emerged from the students, and splendid singing. I had the pleasure of being Chairman, and introducing all those acts. There were many clubs, sporting or serious, to appeal to wide-ranging tastes. There was also a club which the mature students of our year 'invented', The Kerensky Club. Alexander Fedorovich Kerensky (1881–1970) was a Russian statesman and lawyer. He was a moderate Socialist, elected to the Fourth Duma (Parliament) in 1912, at the age of 31. He was opposed to the Czarist Government, and joined the Socialist Revolutionary Party. During 1917, the year of the 'Revolution', Kerensky held several Government posts. From Minister of Justice in February he moved to Minister of War and Navy in May, and to Prime Minister in July 1917. He was ousted by the Bolsheviks in November 1917. He lived his last 53 years in exile, first in France, then in Australia and finally (from 1946 to 1970) in the United States of America. All the men and women in the Kerensky Club saw themselves as some sort of exiles, and were nostalgic, emotional and eccentric. There were more men than women in the Kerensky Club, and we had a grand luncheon at the end of every term, with keg cider, exotic food (Chinese, Indian, etcetera) and long sad speeches. A variety of very eccentric toasts were called and drunk. It was all good fun three times a year.

An important part of our course was teaching practice at Bristol schools, often for several weeks at a time. I taught in comprehensive schools at Henbury, Hengrove, and Hartcliffe, and found the massive teaching factories difficult. It was difficult to find the classrooms, then difficult to marshal the troops, and difficult to establish any rapport in such a disjointed regime. I also taught at St. Mary Redcliffe School, adjacent to the famous Bristol church, praised by Queen Elizabeth I. The pupils at that school were 75% 'high flyers' from all over Bristol, and 25% local children. It made for a very unusual atmosphere. One went from classes of clever, committed students to classes who had little or no interest in learning. It was like going from a hot bath to a cold one. It was little wonder that one shivered. The other school I taught at was Patchway High School, north Bristol and two things about those weeks were memorable. First, it had the most effective disciplinary system I have ever seen. If pupils were at all disruptive the teacher was obliged to send them to the school Secretary, who noted name, class and offence. They were then sent to a large drab room with old desks, old sets of books and two teachers (by rota) always on duty. They then worked all school hours on hard-driven dull work, like a mental treadmill. It made them realise how much better off they were in their own class, doing more interesting work. The other reason I remember Patchway High School was for the student who transported me to and from the school. She was training to teach Business Studies, and her route passed my home road, so we shared transport for weeks. Her name was Diana Beaumont, and her husband Michael was an aircraft engineer at one of Bristol's great aviation companies. He was also the grandson of the famous Dame of Sark, who defied the Nazi occupation of her Channel Island. He was his grandmother's heir, and then she died. It made him and Diana take a great decision. They gave up their Bristol home, jobs and friends to become Seigneur and Dame of Sark, where they have been for about thirty years. The finances of Sark are so complex that Diana's College studies must have stood her in good stead. I often think of that feudal island and its rulers, and the quiet non-motorised lifestyle (except that The Queen visits them by helicopter) and then I think of that modestly successful Bristol couple who were projected into power. As in so many aspects of my own life, truth turns out to be stranger than fiction. How many front lawns does the Queen land on?

In 1976, my penultimate year at Redland College, my book *Sanctions* was published, named for my poem about the Unilateral Declaration of Independence of South Rhodesia from the British Commonwealth, which was punished by Sanctions. My poem is not about politics, and it has proved so popular that it is a major factor in the book selling 60,000 copies in the past 31 years.

After I completed my teaching studies in 1977, I was so disillusioned with the comprehensive school system that I decided to go into adult teaching, but not under the shadow of N.A.T.F.H.E. (National Association of Teachers in Further and Higher Education). I needed to be doing traditional teaching. Fortunately, I had many contacts and past events in colleges throughout the West Country and beyond, and I had no difficulty in organising courses in Bristol and Bath, plus days and events further afield. I eventually offered 34 different courses of any length that a college wanted one day a week – ten weeks, eight weeks, six weeks, four weeks, two weeks, and, at some colleges, residential weekends. My fees were not part of any State budget, and I controlled the entire syllabus of every course. I gave twelve years of such courses before I left Bristol. They were always full (and had a waiting list) and the student response was always one hundred percent. The courses that I offered (at any length) were: Shakespeare, John Dryden, Alexander Pope, William Wordsworth, Alfred Tennyson, John Keats, Robert Southey, Lord Byron, Robert Burns, John Donne, S.T. Coleridge, Matthew Arnold, The Romantic Poets, Robert and Elizabeth Browning, The Rossettis, Longfellow's *Hiawatha*, Emily Dickinson, Robert Frost, Thomas Hardy, W.B. Yeats, Rudyard Kipling, G.K. Chesterton, Hilaire Belloc, John Betjeman, Charles Causley, Dylan Thomas, T.S. Eliot, Philip Larkin, William Blake, The War Poets, A.E. Housman, Louis McNeice, *The Rubaiyat of Omar Khayyam* (Fitzgerald) and P.B. Shelley.

The college where I did most courses was only half a mile from my front door. It was Stoke Lodge Adult Education Centre, on the S-bend of Parry's Lane, Bristol. Stoke Lodge has played a rich part in Bristol education, and the dedication of its staff and students is a heart warming experience. Some years before my literary courses at Stoke Lodge, I was involved in drama, at Bristol Arts Centre, at Bristol University, at the Redgrave Theatre and at Kelvin Players. Some remarkable drama teachers, Barbara Macrae, Eileen Hartly Hodder and Sally Noble had taught hundreds of students the best of drama and verse speaking. Also,

141

in Sally Noble's case, the joys of sight-reading plays not previously seen. She had done many years of drama sight-reading at Stoke Lodge when she asked me to take over from her. I was honoured and delighted, and did many years of twenty weeks a year, autumn and winter. I had a ticket to obtain four sets of plays (up to forty copies of each, as necessary) from Bristol Central Library. I then enrolled thirty students (again, with a waiting list) from either side of Stoke Lodge. On one side was Stoke Bishop, Bristol's most expensive suburb, where the students were often rich or retired people from forty years to eighty years. One man was a 'Master in Lunacy', a retired lawyer who assessed criminal responsibility. The other side of Stoke Lodge was the Seamills Housing Estate, and half my students (for all courses) came from there. They had a passion for learning, and I had a passion for teaching. During two decades I had a wonderful group of sight-readers who could absorb the essence of a play, and play the parts with great skill. It is an exciting exercise. Learning and teaching are both exciting exercises, and I have enjoyed the best of them for more than half a century.

ABERFAN ENQUIRY

How could we know
The spring was underneath?
We do not build
Death-coloured
Heaps of death
On water springs.

How could we tell
The spring was underneath?
We build our heaps of filth,
But save our breath
For higher things.

But all the time
The spring was underneath.
And how do we
Distinguish
Act of God
From act of man?

We realised
The spring was underneath
When it was
Far too late
To stem the tide.
A mountain ran.

What if a spring
Is always underneath?
And under
Every little mound of death
A spring of life?

CONVERSATIONS

Things we have lost? I'll sadly tell you one –
The Art of Conversation. O, what fun
To give whole days to ponder and discuss
The way the whole World was and is to us.
Talks shorter than ten hours have scarce begun!

COMPUTER DATING

Leave nothing now to chance, for your reward
Is Mate and checkmate, if you can afford
Computer-chosen perfect Brides and Grooms.
What is that noise that echoes through the rooms?
"RETURN TO SENDER. DID NOT SAY HE SNORED."

NOT SO HOT FOODSTUFF

I distrust chefs who use too many spices,
Regardless whether high or low their prices,
For spices are not just a taste collection
But have some very practical connection
With fish, flesh, fowl that has gone past its crisis.

TEN MINUTES A DAY

Whether it's breakfast, dinner, merely lunching
Why cook, why sit, why over-stovely hunching,
Why not pack all we need, for good, 'gainst ills
Into thrice-daily Balanced Diet Pills?
Time's far too precious to be spent on munching.

18

Not One Pomeranian Grenadier

My earliest travel was by bicycle, into Surrey and Kent, in the sidecar of a tandem. In later years I bicycled the roads and lanes of those counties, and every other mainland county in England, Scotland and Wales, plus the Isle of Wight and the Isle of Man. I did not quite achieve the 300,000 cycle miles that is the start point for the Long Distance Record Club. If you think that 300,000 pedalled miles is a huge distance (twelve times round the Equator), the present solo bicycle distance is about THREE TIMES 300,000 miles, and may well reach a million miles in a few years time.

From age 30 to age 70 I was a motorist also, which greatly reduced my bicycle use. I drove 400,000 miles without even incurring one parking offence. At age 70, I voluntarily gave up driving. I have only ever travelled by train for work journeys and practical purposes. From age 11 to 25 years, I used London commuter trains with quarterly season tickets, usable without limit into London termini. The cost of all that limitless train travel was about £1 per week.

I have only ever flown in DC3 Dakota aeroplanes to the Isle of Guernsey, two flights each way. A very low carbon imprint. I have no experience of jet aeroplanes.

Hundreds of my happiest days of travel have been by motor coach, all over Britain, and in several European countries. My wife and I reserve our rear seats on the near side, and we ride high above the road, free to look at the country, villages, towns and cities as we pass by. During four decades we have done tens of thousands of miles of coach travel in Britain, France, Belgium, Luxembourg, Germany, Austria and Italy. In our early years of coach travel, it was the incredible cheapness of Continental coach holidays that appealed, but better coaches and better hotels abroad

145

are still cheaper than comparable home travel. I do not know how two-week coach holidays in Europe even cover their cost, let alone profit. In the 1970s, exchange rates in Continental currencies were fantastically favourable, and even in the 1980s one could get huge amounts of continental currency per pound sterling. Forty years ago one could get a week half board in an Austrian town, including all ferry costs and all coach costs (Britain and Europe) and a coach courier for less than £100. Did that even cover the cost of diesel fuel? Only twenty years ago my wife and I entertained two American guests to a two-hour evening meal in pricey Paris, with wine and coffee included for £20 total for the four large meals, including gratuity. Paris cuisine, for less than £5 per person.

But it was not only the extreme economy that appealed to us, but the special ambience of so many European locations. We fell in love with France (not the French); we adored Austria, Bavaria, Bruges, and northern Italy, Venice, Verona and Lake Garda. We went to all of those places by coach, Austria many times, Bruges several times, and northern Italy several times. And there were all the marvellous towns and cities in France, Germany, and Italy where we stayed in transit. Twice on cheap tours we have stayed in French chateaux. Twice for an Austrian fortnight we stayed in lakeside castles, at less cost than Cumbria or York would be. (We were fortunate in Cumbria that our friends and neighbours, the Baileys, gave us a cottage for weeks at a time.)

Bruges was near enough for four or five days to be worthwhile. More than once we travelled via Zeebrugge on the *Spirit of Free Enterprise* when the car deck doors were properly closed. More poet luck. We got to know special places in Bruges, special shops and restaurants, and the historic sites and galleries and concerts. The horse-drawn tour of the city was always a delight, and visiting the superb collection of ancient crested coaches. All our hotels were in the heart of Bruges, and no greater cost than quality B & B in Britain. They never made any profit out of us. One Sunday in Bruges, Jean and I bought tickets for a chamber music concert by the Heidelberg Chamber Orchestra. It was held in a former church, capable of holding hundreds of people. On the day there were fewer than 50 audience, and the conductor invited us all into front rows. That required removal of large numbers of printed RESERVED cards. The local musical supporters paid large subscriptions to secure visiting artists, but did not attend! That would have been asking too much of them. It was a wonderful and exciting concert.

Brittany (ferry to St. Malo) was another of our favourite European places. We had friends at St. Brieuc, and they took us all over Brittany during holidays at their home. Their children were at Rennes and Nantes universities, two charming cities, and Mont-St. Michel, Dinard, Dinan, Brest and The Granite-Rose-Coast were other places we visited. Also Plouha (of the 'Danse Macabre' frieze in the church), and Yffiniac, home village of Bernard Hinault, five times winner of the Tour de France. In the land of the Loire we also saw Angers, and Chateaubriant, named after a famous French author who has a memorial island for his tomb. Authors are very well remembered in France, with streets, squares and boulevards named after them in many towns and cities. Poets like Lamartine and Eluard have their names all over France, like Tennyson and Wordsworth in England, or Burns in Scotland.

Normandy was another region we visited from Granville in the south to Caen and Bayeux and all the beaches of 1944 'D-Day' invasion of Europe. At Bayeux we saw the famous tapestry (1066–1077) of the Norman Conquest of England, and at Caen the separate abbeys where William the Conqueror and his wife were buried. We also sampled the Calvados apple-based spirit, and the superb soft cheese 'Pont L'Eveque' (Bishop's Bridge). The sea off the 1944 invasion beaches still has rusty remnants of the Mulberry Harbour and pipe line under the ocean (PLUTO) on which Jean's father was a Senior Engineer. The invasion museums, and the memorials are unforgettable to people our age (70+).

Apart from three visits to Paris, and two weeks at Mimizan-La-Plage, halfway between Bordeaux and Biarritz, on the Atlantic Coast of Les Landes, our other French holidays were on the Côte d'Azur, Cannes, Nice, Antibes, Renoir's Cagnes-sur-Mer, Monaco, Monte Carlo and Menton. Inland were Vence, rich artists' town, and Grasse (the place of Perfumes) where Queen Victoria often wintered. We were in Monaco and Monte Carlo only weeks before Princess Grace died in a car crash on the mountain. That summer (1982) had seen Mafia wars all along that coast, and Grace's death may have been 'assisted'. Similar things were being said fifteen years later (1997) about the death of Princess Diana in Paris. In the Alpes Maritimes there are some wonderful high places associated with the Knights Templar.

Except for two weeks in Bavaria, our German journeys were mostly transits to Austria. Places where we stayed in Germany were Saarbrucken, Cologne, Stuttgart, and Rothenburg (two weeks). At the end of July 1983 we were in Saarbrucken on the hottest night since 1859 (124 years before). It had been 38°C during the day, and was 30°C at midnight. Jean tried to sleep in an ice-cold towel, while I walked through town to the bridge over the River Saar, and spent the night hours in a wine bar with ten nationalities of insomniacs. The following day, 100 miles south, the storm broke in very spectacular style, with sheet lightning, forked lightning and torrential rain. The storm lasted about two hours, and the temperature fell 15 degrees Celsius. We glimpsed places we would later visit, Cologne with its magnificent cathedral and Roman/German Museum; Bonn (when it was still the seat of West German government); Frankfurt; Heidelberg; Stuttgart; Ulm; the two Ammergaus (Ober and Unter) and Garmisch Partenkirchen, just north of the Austrian border. Under the shadow of the Zugspitze mountain we left Germany with its smart border guards with huge pistol holders, and were welcomed by cigarette-smoking, shirt-sleeved, hand-of-cards Austrians. In twenty border crossings no Austrian entered our coach. At least one German guard always did, sometimes two. Wörms and

Heidelberg (home of Mark Twain) were very special cities, and the VAST statue(s) at Wörms of the masters of the Protestant Reformation are worth a visit any day. Alongside the great rivers, Rhine and Danube, were other memorable places, Rudesheim (home of the truly deafening Drosselgasse (street) and Music Museum), Assmanshausen (the Rhine's only red wine), and Boppard, the ferry of the young lovers in the wonderful (11 hours) film *Heimat* (One). Nothing fails like success. Heimat Two I found totally unintelligible. One two-week tour we travelled the 'Romantische Strasse' from Wurzburg and Nurnberg in the north, to Regensburg (Marcus Aurelius Imperial City), Augsburg, and Rothenburg-on-Tauber, where we stayed at the ancient Bell Inn. Regensburg is the city of Don John of Austria, for whom see G.K. Chesterton's famous poem 'Lepanto' (the last sea battle with rowed ships). The twenty-four-year old triumphant admiral (in command of three fleets) was promoted to govern The Low Countries and then poisoned by the jealous relative who promoted him. Don John was born in Regensburg (on Danube) but had to wait 400 years for a statue. I copied out the (all in Latin) inscription on it. Regensburg also has the quayside restaurant that has been continuously open 1,400 years. Rothenburg is that great rarity, a totally walled city, most of the walls rebuilt after World War Two, by donations from abroad.

South of the border, in Austria, is my magic Tyrol and Innsbruck, city of Maximilian and Maria Theresa, mother of sixteen children while being Empress (in her spare time). Her 1780 silver dollars are still minted for sale, and I have a few of them. Little works of art. My wife and I have been back and back and back to Austria. It is our (non-ageing) Shangri-La. An ideal circular tour starts at Innsbruck and heads east via Jenbach, Mayrhofen, Seefeld ('Langlauf', flat ski centre), Salzburg, St. Wolfgang and St. Gilgen, Strobl, St. Johan in Tirol, Kitzbuhel. A quick look at Graz and Linz (boyhood of Hitler), Vienna and Carinthia (The Lakes). Then back west to Innsbruck, where the long viaduct climbs to the Brenner Pass and into north Italy, where most places have two names (e.g. Vitpiteno and Sterzing) because all north Italy used to be part of Tyrol territory. One of our best fortnights ever was at the tiny village of Steinach-am-Brenner, under the shadow of the mountains hiding Italy. From homely 'Zimmer-Frei' houses to huge Schloss hotels (such as the Eibenstein at St. Wolfgang) we have enjoyed every aspect of Austria (except the snow) in every month from April to September. We have friends there, especially at Sellrain, in the suburbs of Innsbruck. Part of our hearts will always be there. Everywhere I went I read my poetry and sold my books. My reading at Hotel Schloss Eibenstein was given on a ballroom stage where the Strausses played, under life-size portraits of Emperor Franz Josef and his Empress Elisabeth. I also sold 88 books at that reading. The 4000 schillings raised bought treats and presents for us and all the family. We never got to Mayerling, where Rudolf, only son of Franz Josef and Elisabeth, died in 1888, with his teenage lover Maria Vetsera. Because of Rudolf's death, a substitute heir, Archduke Ferdinand, was found. He was assassinated in the streets of Sarajevo in July 1914, leading to World War One. It was a Balkan revolution. An earlier and wiser German General declared "The whole of The Balkans is not worth the blood of one Pomeranian Grenadier". Such wisdom would have avoided a war.

Finally we turn south, over the Brenner Pass and into Italy. Merano, Bolzano, Trento (scene of the Great Church Council (1545 to 1563)), Riva del Garda, Limone, Brescia, Verona, Padua and Venice. We have wonderful memories of all those places where we went several times (chauffeur-driven by coach) at different seasons. Our special holiday places were Limone-sul-Garda, Riva del Garda, and Verona. The others were day journeys in days of storm and sunshine. The afternoon breeze makes the north end of Lake Garda a world centre for wind-surfing – hundreds of bright butterflies skimming the surface. Seen from a sun-lounger at the lakeside it is an exotic sight. Seen from a lake steamer it is breath-taking as they skim under the bows of the ship and away again. A rainbow-show (but rather them than me).

But no Italian memory equals our best of Austria, spring in Salzburg, midsummer in Mayrhofen, autumn at St. Wolfgang, living in the Castle and lunching in the famous White Horse Inn at the side of the beautiful Wolfgangsee. But always we return to Innsbruck, in its walls of mountains, beside its bubbling river, where the tall monument of Maria Theresa and the Golden Roof (real gold) of Maximilian are only two of a hundred special things. Innsbruck repays all the time you give it.

My wife and daughters are much more adventurous travellers than I am. In addition to the places already mentioned, they have been, by jetplane, ship or train to Canada, Holland, Prague, Rome, Florence, Barcelona, Madrid, Carvoeiro, Cyprus, Rhodes, Crete, Tunisia, Israel, Jordan, Egypt and Malta. Jean has been to several European Christmas markets at Valkenburg, Aachen, Trier, Salzburg, Prague...

My daughters, Jane and Ann, were 'backpackers' in their student years, in France, Germany, Austria, Spain, Portugal, Greece and the Balkans. Jane stays in Switzerland with friends, and Ann has done cake art demonstrations in Holland, Germany, Cyprus and the U.S.A., where her videos and books are as popular as in the UK. I stay home and worry about them, until they return.

COUNTY CRICKET MATCH

It wasn't merely that the game was slow,
Nor that the players wouldn't "have a go",
But every time my eyelids uncongealed
I simply saw the fielders cross the field.
Mad for excitement, I observed grass grow.

CIVIL WAR (BRITISH)

Our clipped emotions, non-committal Art
Reveal that we are being torn apart,
For all our feelings falteringly blend
Because OUR Civil War will never end.
We're Royalists for show, Roundheads at heart.

CIVIL WAR (AMERICAN)

No legislation, Gettysburg Address
Will ever clear the masochistic mess
That's called UNITED. Though the same sun swelters
Damn Yankees and the bigot Bible Belters
They do not hate each other any less.

VIENNESE WINTER-MAN

No wonder Sigmund Freud attracts such loathing;
He stole our innocence, and gave us nothing.
He told his frozen patient, snow-soaked through,
"You're not cold, wet; nothing you think is true.
That's not bad weather, just ill-chosen clothing."

JESTING PILATE

Telling the truth is a costly business.
Costly things are also rare.
Few set out on a truthful journey
Being unwilling to pay the fare.
But most have found, before reaching twenty,
That if you wish to press honest views
You must opt out of the land of plenty.
Truth is for those with nothing to lose.
Pilate certainly wasn't jesting
When "What is truth?" was tiredly uttered.
He knew on whose throne his rear was resting.
He knew which side his bread was buttered.
But, because he knew what the truth demands,
He took some water, and washed his hands.

ONE WAY LONDON

Plumbing is part of being civilised.
Or is it? Was it pipes and cisterns that
Raised ancient Romans somewhere near the Greeks?
Does being civilised mean, without leaks?
Pipe to the concourse ditties of revolt,
Pipes full of holes from which sweet sounds leak out,
Crossroads with choice, and squares where one may sleep
Parks full of peace, and not one roundabout.
What's your collective word for contumely?
Eliot's dead that traverse London Bridge?
Ants in an anthill? Bees within a hive?
Leemings a-leaping? Elvers in a tide?

Not even animals that hunt in herds.
Great London Cistern flushes all its turds.

19

I Do Like To Be Beside The Seaside

In 1773 the famous author and reformer Hannah More stayed at Rose Cottage, Uphill, a village to the south of present-day Weston-super-Mare. She was then 28 years old, and beginning to be famous. By coincidence (?) the Rev. Dr. John Langhorne, then 38-years old, was also staying nearby. They met while walking on the beach, and he wrote in the sand with his walking stick:

"Along the shore walked Hannah More; Waves, let this record last; Sooner shall Ye, proud earth and sea, Than what SHE writes, be past."

In reply, with her parasol, Hannah wrote in the sand:

"Some firmer basis, polished Langhorne, choose To write the dictates of thy charming Muse; Her strains in solid characters rehearse, And be thy tablet lasting as her verse."

Hannah had French, Italian, Spanish, Latin and Mathematics skills, and that same year (1773) published *The Search for Happiness*, a pastoral play for schools. Was she in Uphill searching for happiness? Was he? Their paths diverged again, and in 1774, Dr. Langhorne wrote his most famous work, *The Country Justice*, much praised by Wordsworth, who was inspired by it to his own great works. Also in 1774, Hannah More went to London, and lived with the Garricks, and became one of the original 'Blue Stocking Circle' of clever women. Hannah's friends included Edmund Burke, Dr. Samuel Johnson, Samuel Richardson, Sir Joshua Reynolds, and Mrs. Elizabeth Montague (Dr. Johnson's 'Queen of the Blues'). Hannah's tracts sold two million copies in four years, and led to the foundation of the Religious Tract Society in 1799.

Langhorne and More were among the leading minds of the 18th century, and where did they go for rest and recreation? Uphill! It is where my Jean taught for four years, it is where our granddaughter Jasmine is now at 'Grandma's School', and it is where I used to go in the 1950s to meet Jean out of school. I had better luck than Langhorne. Fifty years later, Jean and I would still choose Uphill for rest and recreation. It is where William Lisle Bowles, son of the Rector of Uphill (1769-1786), wrote his famous *Fourteen Sonnets* that inspired the Romantic authors to transform English poetry. W. L. Bowles died in 1850, and, in old age, visited his boyhood coast, and wrote about the old Saint Nicholas Church, upon the hill, "My father came, the pastor of this church That crowns the high hill crest, above the sea; When, as the wheels went slow, and the still night seemed listening, a low murmur met the ear, Not of the winds; my mother softly said, Listen! It is the Sea!....."

By 1850, the collection of cottages north of Uphill had become a seaside resort. Just as Brighthelmstone in Sussex begat Brighton, and as the south end of Prittlewell in Essex spawned Southend, so Uphill inspired Weston. (If the folk at Worle say otherwise, just thump 'em.) Posher than Brighton or Southend, Weston added two LATIN words, and all the snobs of Bristol and Somerset and beyond beat a popular path to Weston SUPER MARE. Things went on quite well for about one hundred years. But in the 1960s The Beatles lowered the tone of Weston, and in each decade the town faded and peeled a bit more, a few more small special shops closed, and a few big attractions ceased to be.

Then, at the end of 1990, decline became fall. Bill and Jean Pickard moved to Weston for their retirement years. The ideal place to go for one's retirement is the seaside near to where you spent your fifties and sixties. Especially if your children and grandchildren are there. So there was no question where we would seek a place for our declining decades. But we had to be within easy bus distance of our friends at Bristol, and Taunton is a favourite day outing, so every consideration pointed to Weston. We wanted a slower pace of life, an easier house to run, and, hopefully, everything within walking distance. In 1989/90 house price inflation was near its peak, and our 1964 purchase had upvalued by twenty times. Buyer interest was frenzied. The valuations by different agents varied by £40,000. Some said £180,000, and we had people call on us with cheque book and pen in hand, willing to pay £18,000 deposit. That was BEFORE they had viewed it. But we wanted to do the right thing. We eventually sold to a young couple with two sons who would benefit from the Elmlea schools. We 'lost' £40,000, but we helped a young family. We had paid £7,000 in 1964 and we got £140,000, exactly twenty times what we paid.

At Weston, we were searching for a bungalow, but people in Weston bungalows were staying put. So we found a flat. Our daughter Ann found it for us, and Jean was captivated by her first impression. I went to view it, and was stunned speechless. The flat was HUGE, one whole floor of a Victorian mansion. It had a forty-foot long hall, with two huge dayrooms to the west, and three large bedrooms to the east. It had a garden, a garage and a large forecourt. The hall was lit by eight stained-glass windows and three cut-glass chandeliers. And the owners only wanted £72,000 for the flat. We gratefully agreed. On 26th October 1990 we moved to our apartment knowing that it required some improvement. We had over £60,000 profit from our sale. We had the flat entirely rewired, and entirely replumbed, and entirely redecorated and entirely recarpeted, and we still had £40,000 to spend, or save or invest. It made the last ten years of the second millennium very comfortable and carefree for us. It was a lovely flat to live in and to entertain in. Twenty-four people often sat down at our refectory tables, and we sometimes had thirty to dine. Quite large literary meetings fitted easily into the main day room, where one wall comfortably carried twenty-eight pictures. The big bay window looked out over Weston Bay to Brean Down. There was limitless space and storage. We thought that we would stay there for ever, but we reckoned without our twelve years of physical slowing down. By summer 2002 our bodies would not tolerate the steep hill approaches from town or the seafront.

The twelve years that we lived in the flat were among the most interesting of our lives. We had great involvement with the visual arts, the literary arts and many social activities. Jean graduated 'Higher National Diploma' in Fine Arts at Weston College, in a splendid ceremony at the parish church, followed by high jinks, food and drinks. Our apartment regularly hosted University of The Third Age literature courses, The Circle In The Square poets, and seven years of monthly John Betjeman Society meetings. I also organised twelve annual poetry competitions for the county of North Somerset, from 1991 to 2002, and more than 4,000 poems were entered for those competitions. From 2003 onward my Poetry Cup, in honour of my father, is awarded at the Weston Youth Arts Festival. Another regular activity, at the Royal Hotel, was the Weston and Somerset Music Hall Society, organised by Malcolm and Shirley Rowley. It was a well-attended society that attracted many variety stars of stage, radio and television. A spin-off from the Music Hall Society was the founding of an Annual Clowns Festival, very popular with many. It is a sad fact that I have always been allergic to clowns in any shape or form, indoors, outdoors or in a tent. I am sure that all clowns are worried about my lack of support and enthusiasm. Perhaps that is why the Operatic Clown in *I Pagliacci* is so miserable? For five years I did a monthly poetry evening (with songs by Eric Brooker) at the Royal Air Force Association hotel on Beach Road. Great fun.

The Annual Weston Arts Festival has been one of my major interests for seventeen years, and this year I give my seventeenth Dauncey's Hotel Poetry Day, seven hours of poetry and refreshment. The Festival annually attracts about fifty events, from mid-September to mid-October. The only two founders of the festival still active are Rosemary Dowie and myself. Apart from performers, there are many people who have made Weston Arts Festival possible. They do not appear on stage. They ARE the stage. So many stages in Weston and nearby carry the events. Theatres, churches, church halls, libraries, the museum, hotels, and even parts of town have had events. If there had been a barn we would have 'barnstormed', as the actors, dancers and singers of old used to do. (An adapted barn can be a wonderful venue, like the historic one at Bishops Cleeve, Cheltenham, where I have done many poetry events. This is a hint to any North Somerset farmer who may have a redundant barn?) As with most arts festivals, a few professionals are augmented by a small army of amateurs, and the organisation is continuous from year to year. Like London's Windmill Theatre, we never closed (so far). As I write this, the small army is planning and preparing the 2007 Festival for Verbal, Musical, Dance, Visual and Puppet performances. Few amateur companies can afford to use Weston's Playhouse Theatre for their productions, but a few have graced the Festival. In September 2006 the world-famous poet and comedienne Pam Ayres was our star event, and our guest at a reception. Her books, audio and video tapes have sold by millions. I even have a wall poster of her famous poem about caring for one's teeth!

The words "caring for'" remind me that Weston is "not what it was". Quite apart from maintenance and appearance, Weston has lost many special shops even during the seventeen years that I have been here. At least ten shops where I regularly bought have closed forever. Extrapolate that to everybody's interests, and God knows how many shops and businesses have closed? Weston's Grand Pier is a social and commercial triumph, but the historic Birnbeck Pier is in danger of disappearing below the waves forever. It has long been too dangerous for the public to approach it. How do you make a pier disappear? By neglecting it. Knightstone Pier is in process of re-invention. The results remain to be seen in the long term. The unique TROPICANA Lido is a scene of dereliction. If we ever get a development on acceptable terms, Tropicana will rise again. Do not hold your breath. Even world-famous Blackpool is alleged to be on its last legs, last gasp, (and last throw of the dice?). If a visitor to Weston wants to see what can be achieved by a developer, the new ROZEL has replaced a terribly tired hotel of the same name. Friends who live in the building tell me that it is very good. It is also reviving its area. Perhaps the whole of the Severn Estuary is "thinking too small". There have been seventy years of plans for a hydro electric barrage from Brean Down to Wales. One of the plans is entirely privately funded. It remains just a plan. "Come back Isambard Kingdom Brunel, all is forgiven." Millions of (lesser crested) humans are being held to ransom by greater crested newts, and even smaller creatures. Weston's Civic Society does a good job on a small scale, but where is the large scale vision? Where there is no vision, the people perish. (But greater crested newts survive and thrive.)

More positive places in Weston are the college and Weston General Hospital. Weston College is now on several sites and still growing. Long may it thrive. Weston General Hospital has huge benefits for the whole area, but (like the whole of the National Health Service) it is always financially stressed. It is a wonder that it achieves so much for so many people.

Local politics in Weston are the same mish-mash as local politics anywhere. Every party has some dedicated councillors, and some total 'wastes of space'. In between are workhorses who wonder why they ever got involved. Weston Town Hall is the focus of all North Somerset decisions, some of them alien to Weston-super-Mare. It is a very difficult balancing act. On a smaller scale, there is the town council, based at Grove House, and local in scope. All British politics is in a strange state. The death of the old Labour Party, and the old Conservative Party leaves a crude consensus. Will there soon be three parties of The Centre? During my seventeen years at Weston, our three Members of Parliament have been an Old Conservative clothes horse, followed by a capable Liberal Democrat (now a Lord) and, at present, a new Conservative who spends time and effort in the town. Such time and effort is commendable. One of my Circle In The Square poets is a councillor who was a much-travelled engineer, with wide experience. Sadly, his devotion to his constituents leaves him very little time for poetry. My polling station is less than fifty yards from my front door, about as far as I would ever go for a political purpose. I always use my vote, out of respect for the hard-won right to vote, but I often think (long term) that Shelley was right: "Poets are the true legislators of mankind".

LIBERATED LADY

She burned her bra
And no-one even looked.
For years she'd washed
And polished,
Cleaned and cooked,
Until, one day,
Her husband went too far –
And, that day, Anna
Burned her beastly bra.

He didn't cry, or cringe
Away in fear,
But said,
In accents tender and sincere,
"Your tits aren't what they used to be
My dear."

It was
The understatement of the week.
She burned her roll-on
In a fit of pique.

HOT BATH

Turn on the taps,
Pull down the blind,
Take off your clothes,
Relax, and find
Yourself again.

Layer by layer,
Skin by skin,
Soil, smut and sweat,
Sorrow and sin
All wash away.

Tears fully conscious
And fears unknown
Melt
Like the marrow of your bone,
And disappear.

Drifting and dreaming,
Lost in the mist;
Mother, lover,
And analyst
Are all surpassed.

Tension all gone.
Doubt all drained.
Paradise lost
Now re-regained.
At peace. At last.

20

Nine Lives

This brief chapter is about a black cat, Elly, a lost life, and seven human beings, myself, my wife Jean, our daughters Jane and Ann, and our grandchildren, Tom, Jasmine and Gemma. Elly has lived with Jean and me since she was two months old. She was born at Yatton, North Somerset in Chlöe's first litter, in the year 1993. By March 1994, Elly was ten months old, and played all over our apartment at Weston-super-Mare. She also had a cat-flap out to the garden, and the big wild world. One morning in early March, Elly was playing hop, skip and jump in the long Hall, I was crouched over my drawing-board, and Jean was out shopping. Toward midday I felt a giant with an iron band gradually tightening it around my chest, until the pain almost took over my left arm completely. I had just enough energy to try to get to the telephone, halfway along the hall, but I blacked out on the carpet before I reached the 'phone. Minutes later I woke up, lying on my back, and staring up into one of the three cut-glass chandeliers. But I was not alone. My nose was being nosed, and my face was being licked by a small black cat, whose four paws were on my chest, which was still in an agony of pain. I shuffled my way to the telephone, and had just summoned an ambulance when Jean arrived home with the shopping bags. She filled a small suitcase with my personal items, and I was whisked away to the new observation unit at Weston General Hospital. I was there about a week, gradually losing the pain, and getting well enough to go home. While I had been away my grandson Tom had been born on 8th March 1994. My birthday is always one day later, and, for the past thirteen years I have had a special regard for Elly the black cat. She is now fourteen years old, and has lost one of her lives in an encounter with a motor car out in the road. She limped and hid for several days, and is now a much more careful cat.

On my second day in the hospital, I had bought a copy of *The Independent* newspaper, and read Keith Patrick's kind obituary of Keith Spencer, of the famous art magazine *The Green Book*, who had been among my Bath acquaintances. Keith Spencer had died (aged only 46) at his desk, presumably of a heart attack like mine. But he didn't have a black cat to save him. Sober (boring) people gaze askance at my indulgence of Elly, but they haven't been given an extra thirteen years of life by a kitten's nudging nose and wet tongue. She is now slow and fat, and mostly sleeps (often on my lap), yet when she 'goes' she will have a garden grave and a splendid send-off.

Jean has three weeks every year when she is two years younger than me. The other forty nine weeks she is only one year younger than me. We are of the same era, the same world, the same mind. Her parents met and married in the 1920s world that my parents had to acclimatize to, but their response to that world was almost opposite. Bill and Irene Goodwin were natural entrepreneurs, and they steadily moved from level to level on the terraced hill of the business world. Bill and Emily Pickard (after their exotic first jobs) settled for safety and certainty. They only had two marital homes in 61 years, but the Goodwins had a dozen homes, and Jean went to many schools, one of them at Piers Court, the Gloucestershire home of the famous novelist Evelyn Waugh. Jean's parents were not Catholics, but all her schooling was by nuns. She has the same great gifts as Maria Von Trapp, the super nun of the 20th century. Whether it is little plants or little humans, Jean can get anything to GROW. Her transition from four years at Long Ashton Research Station (tending tree fruits and bush fruits) to Redland Teacher Training College, tending infant and junior children, was as natural as a seed becoming a shoot becoming a plant becoming a fruit for human benefit. All things about Jean are for human benefit, and I am the one who has most benefited. We started out in four attic rooms with low ceilings, but it became a haven for young and old in the parish, because she is a homemaker, and where she is everyone feels at home. My communication gifts only relate to adults or late teenagers, but Jean is on the wavelength of babies, toddlers, infants and juniors. They know she loves them, and they love her in return. Our daughters, Jane and Ann, have had forty years of all those benefits, and Tom, now thirteen, Jasmine aged six, and two-year-old Gemma all feast on Jean's bounty.

Jane has not had an easy life. She spent much of her early years in hospital or in treatment for asthma. All her great achievements have been won in despite of breathing difficulties, and every day life has been a battle for breath. Her school years, her college years, her teaching years and her varied work for great charities all denote deep determination. Jane's first name is Rosemary, and she has a place in the strong remembrance of many people. It is small wonder that her son Tom shows good potential, and, at thirteen, already has constructive ideas about his future.

Heather Ann is two years younger than Jane, and used to be sat in a cardboard box with only her head showing, so that Jane could teach her all she needed to know. Perhaps it is to Jane's credit that Ann had clear ideas about her future when she was only fifteen. She wanted to fashion food, not routine food, but the most special, cakes and patisserie. It is a demanding career, with up to twelve hours a day at a work table in totally controlled hygienic conditions. After her early City and Guilds studies, Ann worked a year for a Bristol baker, from five a.m. to five p.m. She used to get home so exhausted that she slept for hours before she could even eat. Not deterred by that, she went to North Gloucestershire College, at The Parks in Cheltenham, where she did more City and Guilds Courses in all aspects of bakery, patisserie, and cake decoration. It is for cake decoration that she is now world renowned. While she was a student she entered major competitions, and old bakers (amazed by her avant garde designs) told her "Your day will come". It arrived long since, at least twenty years ago, publicly confirmed when she reached the Grand Final of H.T.V. Bristol "You're The Boss", a demanding elimination test of self-employed entrepreneurs, until only four top tycoons remained. It was infinitely more demanding than B.B.C. TV's "The Apprentice" in recent years. Ann's books, videos, DVDs and equipment are popular in Britain, Ireland and the USA. Tokyo tried to claim her, but she declined. Girls from Tokyo had to come to her at Weston-super-Mare, as have many from other distant places. Her regular customers come from a twenty mile radius of Weston, and some from thirty or forty miles away. It is all the more amazing as her career is done in parallel with mothering her two small girls, Jasmine and Gemma. Their daddy, Mark is very helpful with Ann's many events that involve travel and Exhibitions.

Jasmine was born on 16th March 2001, and now goes to school where Jean taught in the 1950s, Uphill Primary School. She is a serious little girl who loves words and stories, and even the dictionary. Possibly a future Doctor Johnson? Gemma is a 'Christmas Girl' (born 22nd December 2004), and she, too, loves words, and uses them wisely. Her new answer to everything is, "Maybe". A girl can't get wiser than that! She dotes on 'Bob the Builder' (as seen on television) and other cartoon characters. They both of them love a real-life (furry) friend, Muppet, a large gentle dog.

What can one say about Tom, the terrible teenager? He has three bikes, including a Tour de France racer, and is a good cook. He goes to Backwell School, a community school, and is his Grandma Jean's pride and joy, and she has perfect taste. That is a very high note on which to end this chapter.

A 'privatised' railway spokesman said
(of an allegedly improved railway station):

"There was a member of staff who did some painting of the
waiting room to reflect the station's history."

THE HOUSE STYLE

The colour green expressed our pleasant land,
The colour cream the best that used to be,
But both are now deleted, even banned;
'House' blue and red are all that we may see.

Blue is the shade of sorrow. We are sad.
Red is the shade of anger and of hate.
So both express the loss of what we had,
And emphasise our present futile fate.

For decades, when I travelled on those lines,
The trains and stations blended with the scene,
But all 'house stylists' have their dark designs
And call the paying public, "sucker green".

What we get now is glaring paint and faults
And extra time to think on what we've lost,
"Leaves on the line", "wrong snow", and other halts,
And all of it at twenty times the cost!

Why it was ever changed defeats the brain,
Beeching's first savage purge the mystery;
All we have now – lost time and cost and pain
And memories of "the station's history".

FIRST THINGS LAST

Drive round the city
On a summer day,
Sweating and swearing
For somewhere to park.

Drive to the suburb
Where the cemetery
Lies beneath yew trees
Tall and cool and dark.

Stop by a tombstone
Where the mourners grieved;
Look at a name
And misrecall a face.

Trace the inscription.
What has he achieved?
Calmly, triumphantly,
A PARKING SPACE.

21

The End, In Every Respect

There is a great lack of self-esteem about. On all sides one hears demands for 'respect', followed by a strong stink of shattered self-esteem. The two go together like lightning and thunder.

The latest super guru, Professor Howard Gardner of Harvard University, U.S.A., holds that the 21st century will demand much greater 'Respect'. To achieve this we must abandon our loyalty to free speech. WHAT A DIRE AND DANGEROUS PROPOSAL! It is the supreme surrender to the poison of political correctness, the fastest spreading disease of modern times. What about pandemic political correctness? The answer is NOT to pussyfoot around all issues, but to be so strong and open that nothing disturbs you, nor causes you any offence. If something is 'alien' to you, it is to the self-harm of the person who propagates it. No other person can pervert or pre-empt your persona.

The First Amendment of the USA Constitution protects Freedom of Expression. It must be our first concern to be free to express. The new Russia is already falling into all the corruptions of the old Soviet Union. Russians who freely express already get killed, imprisoned or robbed of their rights. Does Professor Gardner want the U.S.A. and the Western World to go the same way? He talks much of 'The respectful mind'. Pussyfooting. Far better is the 'resilient mind', able to absorb any shock, and to laugh at it. Many un-successful dictators are defeated by laughter.

Let all weak whingers for 'respect' be seen for what they are – special pleaders for special favours, totally undeserved. The new need in education is to cultivate latent talent as a proper personal basis for self-esteem. Everyone has innate talents, but most of them get wasted. Everyone should have a vocation, but most of them get missed. A proper future depends on every talent being fully developed, and every vocation being fully recognised. Then, and only then, will we have our Brave New World.

Index

Abbott, Christine (YWCA) 75
ACUMEN, (Literary Journal) 123, 125
Adams, Abe 124
Adie, Kate 121
All Systems Stop 106, 130
Allen and Unwin 120
Allen, G.G. 44
Alleyn, Edward 40
Amiens, France 1, 45, 46
Amis, Kingsley 123
Andrews, E.G. 44
Anquetil, Jaques (T.D.F.) 62
Armstrong, Lance (T.D.F.) 62
Armstrong-Jones, Anthony 55
Army School Of Ammunition (RAOC) 67
Arnold, Matthew 118, 141
Arnolfini Gallery, Bristol 122
Arthur and Lillian, (Leatherhead) 29, 30
Arts Council (of GB) 110
Ashburnham Place, Sussex 101, 102
Auden, W.H. 118
Austria 129, 145, 146, 148, 149, 150, 151
Ayres, Pam 134, 158

Bailey, Claire 96
Bailey, Dr. Ian 96, 146
Bailey, E. Macdonald 61
Bailey, Winifred 96, 146
Baldwin, Stanley 20
Barber, R. Jane 162
Barber, Tom 162, 165
Barnard's Inn (of Court) 41, 50

Barnstaple (WCWA) 133
Barton Seagrave Orangery event 106
Basingstoke (theatre and railway) 67, 68
Battersea Park (F.O.B) 72
Battle of Britain 27
Bavaria, Germany 129, 146, 148
B.B.C. Radio Bristol 83, 121, 122
Beake, Fred 124
Beatles, The 155
Beaumont (Michael and Diana) 140
Beaverbrook, Lord 20, 28, 29, 30, 31, 37
Becket, Thomas à 41
Beeton, Mrs (Domestic Goddess) 18
Belloc, Hilaire 141
Bennett, Roger 121
Benson, Percy 45
Bessemer, Sir Henry 18
Betjeman, Sir John 52, 77, 85, 111, 134, 141, 157
Bevan, Aneurin 130
Bible Society 86
Bickersteth, Rev. John 101
Bielski, Alison 123, 124
Billington, Lady Rachel 131
Bishops Cleeve, Cheltenham 158
Blackman, Honor 75
Blake, William 40, 41, 118, 141
Blezard, William 75
B.O.A.C. 55, 78
Boaler, Mrs 103
Boat Races (University) 18
Bowles, Rev. W.L. 155
Bramley, Hants (RAOC) 67
'Bramley Seedlings' (Drama) 67
Bristol Arts Centre 105, 109, 112, 125, 133, 141
Bristol Cathedral (Anglican) 82, 85
Bristol Cathedral (R.C.) 82

170

Bristol Cathedral School 110
Bristol Central Library 110, 142
Bristol Old Vic Theatre 122
BRISTOL POETRY (600 Years of) 110, 111, 112, 138
Bristol University 83, 84, 122, 137, 138, 141
BRISTOLIANA 54
'Britain Can Make It Exhibition' 72
Browning, (Robert and Elizabeth) 141
Bruges, Belgium 146
Burbage, Richard 40
Burns, Robert 141, 147
Burton, (Beryl and Charles) 61, 62
Byron, Lord George 118, 141

Cadogan Square, Chelsea 50
Callaghan, James (PM) 52
Carey, George (Archbishop of Canterbury) 86
Carter, Fred 69
Carter, Sidney 76
Causley, Charles 82, 121, 134, 141
Cavendish, Lady Elizabeth 77
Chamberlain, Neville 22, 23, 26
Chaplin, Charlie 11, 20
Chelsea Arts Ball 78, 122
Chelsea Cloisters 78
Cheltenham (WCWA) 133, 134
Cheltenham Festival of Literature 119
Chesterton, G.K. 141, 149
Christ Church, Gipsy Hill 82, 83
Christie, Agatha 130
Churchill, Winston 20
Circle In The Square 109, 110, 123, 124, 125
Circle In The Square, New York 109
Circle In The Square, poets 109, 110, 118, 122, 124, 125, 157, 159
City Pages 53
Clare, John 118

Clifton Theological College, Bristol 83
Clunies-Ross, Pamela (NPS) 110
Cobbold, Lady Hermione 77
Cobbold, Lord 77
Coleridge-Taylor, Samuel 22
Colston Hall 110, 125
Colston House 105
Comprehensive schools (Bristol) 139
Cooke, Nicole 62
Corgi Transworld 122
Côte d'Azur 148
Croft, Emily Horsley 4
Croft, George Henry Stephen 4
Croft, George Oswald 5
Crystal Palace (the) 11, 13, 18, 20, 21

D Day 147
Dale, Peter (AGENDA) 125
Dalton House, Bristol 86
De La Rue (Printer) 50
Delaney, Frank 131
Denning, Lord (Master of the Rolls) 60
Devereaux (Geographer) 44
Dickinson, Emily 141
Donne, John 118, 141
Doulton, Sir Henry 18
Doves for the Seventies 122
Drabble, Margaret 133
Draper, Prof. N. R. 69
Drop of a Hat (Swann and Flanders) 76
Drop of Another Hat (Swann and Flanders) 76
Dryden, John 118, 122, 141
Du Maurier, Dame Daphne 129, 130
Dulwich College 13, 31, 40
Dulwich Village 40
Dunkirk, France (1940) 26, 27

East Dulwich Hospital 101
Eliot, T. S. 19, 72, 77, 118, 141
Elly (ad. Pickard) 162
Eluard, Paul 147
Eminton, Anne (YWCA) 75
Eton College 101
Eveleigh, Elaine 124
Everest Mountain (1953) 76
Everything By Starts 122
Ewart, Gavin 118
Exeter (WCWA) 130, 131
Ezekiel 58

Fanthorpe, U. A. 118
Farjeon, Herbert and Eleanor 76
Farnham Castle (CACTM) 83
Felix, Julie 122
Festival of Britain (1951) 69, 72
Fetter Lane, London 41
Firth, Barbara (YWCA) 76
Fischer, Frank (KW) 60
Fisher, Lord (Archbishop of Canterbury) 77
Fison, Mr (Mathematics) 44
Fitzgerald, Edward 118, 141
Flanders, Michael 76
Flecker, James Elroy 118
Fonteyn, Dame Margot 103
Foxe's Book Of Martyrs 20
Frost, Robert 141
Fry, Christopher 131

Gaitskell, Hugh 95
Gardner, Prof. Howard 168
Germany 145, 148
Gilbert and Sullivan 10, 68, 95, 117
Gipsy Hill Station 43
Girls of Slender Means 54
Girvan, Waveney (WCWA) 129
GLIMMERICKS 118
Goldsmith, Oliver 118
Good Soldier Schweik, The 65
Goodwin, Bill and Irene 90, 147, 163
Gore, Colonel (Bramley) 67
Gorringes Emporium 42
Görtschacher, Dr. Wolfgang 124
Gowing, William 52
Graham, Winston 131, 132
Grand Prix des Nations (T.T.) 62
Gray, Thomas 118
Great Exhibition (London 1851) 12, 72
Great Yarmouth 2, 3, 7
Grenfell, Joyce 75
Gresham, Sir Thomas 41

Haden, William 49
Half A Ton (BP Selected Poems) 126
Hardy, Thomas 141
Harlech T.V. (Bristol) 83, 164
Harris, Reg 13, 60
Hartly Hodder, Eileen 141
Headland, Rev. James 93
Heaney, Seamus 129
Hemsby, Norfolk 22
Hendry, Diana 125, 133
Henri, Adrian 120
Henty, G.A. 20

Herne Hill Cycle Stadium 13, 59
Herrick, Robert 118
Hess, Rudolf 20
Hiawatha (Longfellow) 22, 141
Hill, A.R.G. (Alf) 59
Hinault, Bernard (TDF) 62
Hippisley Coxe, Anthony 132
Hitchcock, Alfred 132
Hitler, Adolf 20, 23
Hobday, Charles 124
Hogg, James (Ettrick 1770) 14
Hogg, Prof. James (1970) 123, 124
Holborn Viaduct Station 43
Holdsworth, Jack 59
Holdsworth, W.F. (Sandy) 59
Holroyd, Michael 133
Home Office (AJPP) 34
Hood, Thomas 118
Hope, Vida 76
Hopkins, Gerard Manley 54
Horovitz, Frances 125
Horovitz, Michael 125
Horsley, Edith 4
Hotwells Chapel Arts Centre 120
Housman, A. E. 141
Huguenots 1
Hungarian Refugees (1956) 86
Hunt, Chris 124
Hutton, Len 23

Indurain, Miguel (TDF) 62
Ingelow, Jean 118
Innsbruck, Austria 149
Institut Français, London 55
Institute of Personnel Management 105, 137
Isle of Man 61

Isle of Wight 61
Italy 145, 146, 149, 150
Ivy Benson and her Girl Band 78

Jepson, Michael (OMC) 50
Jepson, R. W. (MS) {'Clear Thinking' and 'The Writer's Craft'}
    41, 42, 49
Joan of Arc 62
John o'Groats to Lands End (1953) 59
John, Roland (OUTPOSTS) 123, 124
Johnson, Jenny 124
Jonson, Ben 118
Joy 35, 36, 37, 40, 42
Joy, Ken (cycle record) 59

Kaye, Geraldine (WCWA) 129, 130
Keats, John 22, 118, 141
Kelvin Players, Bristol 141
Kemp-Potter, Joan (Mrs. Wm. Blezard) 75
Kennington Oval (Surrey CCC) 18, 23
Kentish Wheelers 59, 60
Kerensky Club (Redland College) 139
Killingback, Jack (KW) 59
King Edward VIII 19, 20, 21, 26
King George V 2, 19
King George V and Queen Mary 42
King George VI 22, 65
King, Charles OBE (KW) 60
Kipling, Rudyard 19, 65, 118, 133, 141
Korean War 79

Lamartine, Alphonse 147
Lambeth Borough Council 7
Landor, Walter Savage 118
Lands End to John o' Groats (1952) 59
Langhorne, Rev. Dr. John 154

Lara, Brian 23
Larkin, Philip 141
Latham, Arthur Selby 73, 74
Leatherhead, Surrey 28, 29, 30, 34, 42, 137
Lee, Jennie (Baroness Asheridge) 130
Lee, Laurie 132, 133
Leeds 2
Lewis, C.S. 34
Lido Jenny, Hyde Park, London 78
Literary Courses (34 Subjects) 141
LITTLE MAGAZINE PROFILES 124
Little Theatre (Colston Hall) 110
Lively, Penelope (WCWA) 132
Lochhead, Liz 124
London County Council 31, 40
London University 46, 49, 111
Long Ashton Research Station 163
Longes, Rev. Stanley 83
Longfellow, H.W. 22, 141
Loosing My Grip 122
Lord, Mike 105, 109
Lovelace, Sir Richard 118
Lovell, Ryl 124
Lovell, Sir Bernard 110
Lucy and the Hunter (Swann and Carter) 76
Lyle, Lord (of Westbourne) 53, 73
Lyle, Sir Ian 53
Lyle's Golden Syrup 49

Macdonald, George 34
MacNeice, Louis 141
Macrae, Barbara 141
Mandelson, Peter 72
Marples, Ernest 68
Martin, Edward (Teddy) 110
Matthias, Sister 93, 100

Maxim, Sir Hiram 18
Mayne, Rev. Michael 92
McGough, Roger 120
McKechnie, Rev. John 99
McKenzie, G (P.E.) 44
McNaghten, Robin and Petronella 100, 101
Meek, Rev. John Conway 93
Mercers' Company 50
Mercers' Hall, London 50
Mercers' School 17, 30, 31, 41, 43, 44, 49, 137
Merckx, Eddy (TDF) 62
Mercury House, Bristol 105, 109
Mermaid Theatre, London 123
Mersey Poets (The) 120
Merton College, Oxford 83
Milne, A.A. 20
Milton, John 118
Mincing Lane, London 72, 73
Montgomery, Field Marshall 49
Moore, Thomas 118
Moravian Church, Fetter Lane 41
More, Hannah 154
Morrison, Herbert 72
Moss, Stuart 44, 45
Motyer, Rev. Alexander 85
Muggeridge, Malcolm 92
Mulberry Harbour 147
Mumford, Bill 59
Murray, Melissa 124
Museums (British, Science, Victoria and Albert, Imperial War,
    Horniman's) 22
Mussolini, Benito 20
My Fair Lady (Original Cast) 91

Napoleon Bonaparte 65, 66
Nash, Thomas 118

National Nautical School 85
National Poetry Secretariat 110
National Service (RAOC) 65
Newbolt, Sir Henry 118
Newgate Prison, London 41
Newman, Paul 109
Nkrumah, President K. 73
Noble, Sally 141, 142
Normandy, France 147
North Somerset County 119, 157, 158, 159
North Somerset Poetry Competitions 119
Norwood Cemetery 18
Norwood Park 13
Norwood, Bloomfield Estate 17
Norwood, Salters Hill 11, 17, 19
Norwood, Salters Hill School 13, 14, 137
Norwood, South London 6, 7, 11, 17
Norwood, Upper (SE19) 7
Norwood, West (SE27) 10, 17, 18, 43, 84

Obey, André 'Noah' Play 68
Old Mercers' Club 50, 118
Old Vic Theatre, Waterloo Road 69
Olympic Games London 1948 13, 60
Orczy, Baroness 20
O'Shaughnessy, Arthur 118
OUTPOSTS Magazine 55, 111, 123
Outsider, The (Colin Wilson) 35
Owen, Wilfred 118
Oxley, Patricia (ACUMEN) 123, 125
Oxley, William (LITTACK) 123, 125
Palgrave's Golden Treasury 14, 118, 122
Palmer Park Track, Reading 60
Paris, France 146, 148
Parsons Barracks, Aldershot 65, 66
Patchway High School 103, 140

Paternoster, Charles Cosgrove 51
Patmore, Coventry 118
Patrick, Keith 163
Patten, Brian 120
Peake, Mervyn 34
Penguin Modern Poets 120
Penzance (WCWA) 130, 133
Philpotts, Eden (WCWA) 131
Picardie, France 1
Picasso, Pablo 52
Pickard, Albert J. (Senior) 2
Pickard, Group Captain Percy C. 45, 46
Pickard, Group Captain Walter J. 46
Pickard, Heather Ann 104, 132, 151, 162, 164
Pickard, Jean F.E. 90, 99, 100, 151, 154, 155, 162, 163
Pickard, Rosemary Jane 101, 151, 164
Pickard, Sir Benjamin 2
Pickard, William P (Senior) 2, 5, 6, 11, 163
Pickards, Albert, William, John, Donald 2
Pipe Line Under The Ocean (PLUTO) 147
Pirie, Gordon 61
Poetry Review 53
POETRY SCOTLAND 125
Poetry Society 53, 54
Pope, Alexander 118, 141
Post Office (Mercury House) 105
Preston Park Track, Brighton 60
Priestley, John Boynton 5, 6, 26, 27
Princess Margaret 77, 99
PUNCH LINES (B.P.) 54

Quarles, Francis 118
Queen Elizabeth II: Bristol 600 Book 110
Queen Elizabeth II (Coronation) 59, 76
Queen Elizabeth Hall, London 122
Queen Mary (wife of King George V) 42

Queen Mary Hall (YWCA) 55, 68, 75

Raine, Kathleen (TEMENOS) 125
Randles, Leslie 91
Rank, Sir J. Arthur 53
Redcliffe Press, Bristol 122
Redland College, Bristol 112, 129, 137, 138, 140, 163
Regent, The, Brighton 75
Ricks, Professor Christopher 122
River Mole (Fetcham Splash) 35, 36
Roberts, Rev. Llewellyn 84, 85
Robins, Peter (BBC London) 121
Romantic Poets (the) 141, 155
Rossetti, Christina 118, 141
Rossetti, Dante Gabriel 118, 141
Rossetti, Vernon (Mercers' School) 44, 45
Rowley, Malcolm and Shirley 157
Royal Air Force 157
Royal Army Ordnance Corps 65
Royal Hotel, Bristol 131, 133, 134
Royal Navy (AJPP 1940–1946) 34
Rozel, Weston-super-Mare 158
Rubaiyat of Omar Khayyam 122, 141
Russian Orthodox Wedding 75

Sainsbury, Rev. Roger 86
Salamanca, Spain (Battle & Barracks) 65
Salmon, Rev. Richard 92, 102
Salzburg University, Austria 123, 124
Samson, (Judges 14.14) 49
SANCTIONS (60,000 copies sold) 140
Sarajevo, Bosnia 150
Sark, C.I. (Seigneur & Dame) 140
Save the Children Fund 74
Savoy Hotel, Strand, London 74
Scandinavia (B.P. Translations) 54

Schmidt, Michael 124
Schneider, Rev. Peter 94
Scott, Mr. (M.S. Latin) 44
Seamills Housing Estate 142
Seething Lane, London EC 52
Selwyn College, Cambridge 83
Sentamu, Rev. Dr. (Archbishop of York) 102
Sergeant, Howard 54, 111, 123
Shaftesbury (7th Earl) 103, 104
Shaftesbury Crusade, Bristol 103, 104
Shakespeare, William 40, 118, 141
Shaw, George Bernard 45, 109
Shelley, P.B. 118, 141, 159
Shelter (Housing Association) 120
Sheppard, Rt. Rev. D (Bishop of Liverpool) 82
Sherborne School, Dorset 101
Sherriff, R.C. (Journey's End) 69
Shields, Mike (ORBIS) 125
SHORT BACK AND SIDE EFFECTS 118
Simpson, Mrs. Wallis 19, 20, 22
Sir Claude of Southwarke 54
'Skylon', Battersea Park (1951) 72
Smithfield Market V2 45
Snowdon, Earl of 99
Soar, Geoffrey 124
South West Arts, Exeter 130
Southey, Robert 141
Southwark (Diocese and Cathedral) 86, 91, 92, 99
Spark, Muriel 53, 54, 126
Spencer, Keith 163
Spielberg, Steven 117
Spurgeon, Charles Haddon 18, 83
St. George the Martyr 100
St. Helen, Rainham, Essex 102, 103
St. James, Lockleaze 104
St. Mary Magdalene, Bristol 90, 99

St. Mary Redcliffe Church 111
St. Mary Redcliffe School 139
St. Matthias, Upper Tulse Hill 90, 93, 94
St. Nicholas Church Museum, Bristol 111
Stanford, Derek 54
Steane, Nina 106
Stevenson, Robert Louis 117
Stockwood, Mervyn (Bishop of Southwark) 91, 92, 99
Stoke Bishop (Students) 83, 90
Stoke Lodge Adult Education Centre 141, 142
Stoppard, Sir Tom 117
Swann, Donald 76

Tate, Sir George Vernon 52, 53
Tate and Lyle 49, 50, 60, 72, 73, 82, 83, 137
Taunton, Somerset 132, 155
Tennyson, Alfred (Lord) 118, 141, 147
Theokritoff family (YWCA) 75
Thomas, Dylan 117, 141
Thompson, Francis 118
Thompson, Major (RAOC) 67
Thatcher, Margaret and Denis 40, 131
Torquay, Devon (WCWA) 130, 132
Trapnell, Rev. Stephen 93
Trinity College, Bristol 86
Trowbridge College 120, 121
Tropicana, Weston-super-Mare 158
Tulse Hill School 95
Turner, John (BBC) 121
Tussaud, Madame 22
Tyndale Hall College (BCMS) 86
Tyrol, Austria 149, 150, 151

Union Jack Club, Waterloo Road 69
Uphill Primary School 90
Uphill Village, Weston-super-Mare 154, 155

Urchfont Manor (Wiltshire) 111

V1 Rockets, London 1944 46
V2 Rockets, London 1944 45
Vaughan, Henry 118
Verstegan (Palgrave G.T. Poet) 118
Veteran-Cycle Club 58
Victoria Station 19, 79
Voice, Rev. Norman 103
Von Hapsburg, Elizabeth 150
Von Hapsburg, Franz Josef 150
Von Hapsburg, Prince Rudolf 150
Von Trapp, Maria 163
Von Tutschek, Alexander 58

Wainwright, Eddie 129
Wainwright, Verena 129
Wallace, Billy (Wallace Collection) 77
'War and Peace In The Holy Bible' 138
War Graves Commission 19
Wars of the Roses 1
Waterloo Churches (St. John, St. Luke, St. Mark and St. Matthew)
    17
Waterloo Railway Station 68, 69, 100
Watershed, Bristol 113, 114
Watts, Gemma 162, 165
Watts, Jasmine 117, 154, 162, 165
Watts, Mark 165
Wellinton Lines, Aldershot 65
Wells, H.G. 131
Wennington, Essex 102, 103
Wesley, Rev. John 41
West Country Writers Association 129, 130, 134
Westminster Abbey, (Poets Corner) 92
Weston and Somerset Music Hall Society 157
Weston Civic Society 159

Weston College 157, 159
Weston General Hospital 159, 162
Weston Junior Arts Festival 119, 157
Weston-super-Mare 90, 130, 132, 154, 155, 156, 162, 164
Weston, Playhouse Theatre 158
Weymouth, Dorset 133
Wheel And Woe 105
Whitehouse, Dr. (M.S. Biology) 44
Whittington, Sir Richard 41
Williams, Rev. Leslie 99
Williamson, Henry (WCWA) 131
Wilson, Colin (*The Outsider*) 35
Wilson, Lady Mary 92, 111
Wilson, Sandy (*The Boy Friend*) 75
Woodward, Joanne (Mrs Paul Newman) 109
Woolwich, Bishop (John Robinson) 99
Wordsworth, William 14, 96, 118, 141, 147, 154
Worker Priest Movement 104, 105
'Wreck of the Deutschland' poem 54
Wren, Sir Christopher 126

Yeats, W.B. 118, 141
York 4, 45
Yorkshire 1
Young Women's Christian Association 55
YWCA Centenary (Albert Hall) 77
YWCA Drama 55, 75

Zeebrugge (Spirit of Free Enterprise) 146